Revolutions in Book Publishing

Other Palgrave Pivot titles

Dietrich Orlow: **Socialist Reformers and the Collapse of the German Democratic Republic**

Gwendolyn Audrey Foster: **Disruptive Feminisms: Raced, Gendered, and Classed Bodies in Film**

Catherine A. Lugg: **US Public Schools and the Politics of Queer Erasure**

Olli Pyyhtinen: **More-than-Human Sociology: A New Sociological Imagination**

Jane Hemsley-Brown and Izhar Oplatka: **Higher Education Consumer Choice**

Arthur Asa Berger: **Gizmos or: The Electronic Imperative: How Digital Devices have Transformed American Character and Culture**

Antoine Vauchez: **Democratizing Europe**

Cassie Smith-Christmas: **Family Language Policy: Maintaining an Endangered Language in the Home**

Liam Magee: **Interwoven Cities**

Alan Bainbridge: **On Becoming an Education Professional: A Psychosocial Exploration of Developing an Education Professional Practice**

Bruce Moghtader: **Foucault and Educational Ethics**

Carol Rittner and John K. Roth: **Teaching about Rape in War and Genocide**

Robert H. Blank: **Cognitive Enhancement: Social and Public Policy Issues**

Cathy Hannabach: **Blood Cultures: Medicine, Media, and Militarisms**

Adam Bennett, G. Russell Kincaid, Peter Sanfey, and Max Watson: **Economic and Policy Foundations for Growth in South East Europe: Remaking the Balkan Economy**

Shaun May: **Rethinking Practice as Research and the Cognitive Turn**

Eoin Price: **'Public' and 'Private' Playhouses in Renaissance England: The Politics of Publication**

David Elliott: **Green Energy Futures: A Big Change for the Good**

Susan Nance: **Animal Modernity: Jumbo the Elephant and the Human Dilemma**

Alessandra Perri: **Innovation and the Multinational Firm: Perspectives on Foreign Subsidiaries and Host Locations**

palgrave▶pivot

Revolutions in Book Publishing: The Effects of Digital Innovation on the Industry

Lall Ramrattan
Instructor, University of California, USA
and
Michael Szenberg
Distinguished Professor of Economics and Chair of Business and Economics, Touro College and University System, USA

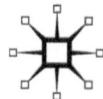

REVOLUTIONS IN BOOK PUBLISHING
Copyright © Lall Ramrattan and Michael Szenberg, 2016.
Foreword © Benjamin M. Friedman, 2016

All rights reserved.

First published in 2016 by
PALGRAVE MACMILLAN®
in the United States—a division of St. Martin's Press LLC,
175 Fifth Avenue, New York, NY 10010.

Where this book is distributed in the UK, Europe and the rest of the world, this is by Palgrave Macmillan, a division of Macmillan Publishers Limited, registered in England, company number 785998, of Houndmills, Basingstoke, Hampshire RG21 6XS.

Palgrave Macmillan is the global academic imprint of the above companies and has companies and representatives throughout the world.

Palgrave® and Macmillan® are registered trademarks in the United States, the United Kingdom, Europe and other countries.

ISBN: 978-1-137-57622-4 EPUB
ISBN: 978-1-137-57621-7 PDF
ISBN: 978-1-137-57620-0 Hardback

Library of Congress Cataloging-in-Publication Data is available from the Library of Congress.

A catalogue record of the book is available from the British Library.

First edition: 2016

www.palgrave.com/pivot

DOI: 10.1057/9781137576217

To my late mother and father-in-law, Sundermonie and Munisamy Munian from Bath Settlement, West Coast Berbice, Guyana. I thank them for their love, enthusiastic encouragement and generous support in words and deeds in my search for knowledge. I wish their souls eternal peace and happiness.
–L.R.

B"H

Dedicated to the memory of my sister, Esther, for bringing me to these shores; to the memory of my parents, Henoch for his wisdom and my mother, Sara, for giving birth to me—twice; to my wife Miriam and my children Naomi and Avi, their spouses Marc and Tova; to my grandchildren, Elki and Chaim, Batya, Chanoch, Devorah and Nachum, Ephraim, Ayala, Jacob, and to my great-grandchildren, Chanoch and Fegila. And to the righteous German officer who took my immediate family to a hiding place just days before the last transport to Auschwitz, where most of my family perished.
–M.S.

Contents

List of Figures	vii
List of Tables	viii
Foreword *Benjamin M. Friedman*	x
Preface and Acknowledgments	xiv
1 General Introduction	1
2 Overview of Price and Nonprice Competition	18
3 Consumption Aspects: Empirical Findings	50
4 Production Aspects: Employment, Manpower, and Productivity	72
5 Distribution Aspects of the Industry	94
6 Printing and Publishing	108
7 Internet Technological Aspects of the Industry	120
Conclusions	131
References	134
Index	146

List of Figures

1.1	Amazon versus Naics 511 R&D, 1998–2007 ($m)	16
2.1	Price and nonprice decisions	19
2.2	Supply and demand for books	32
2.3	Product versus spatial differentiation of the e-book market	37
2.4	Dynamic view of the book industry	39
2.5	The Chain Store Paradox	42
3.1	Book category share, 1985–2002	55
7.1	Outline of issues in Internet technology	123
7.2	Book industry value chain: business to consumer	127

List of Tables

1.1	Industry classification	7
1.2	Long-term growth, 1929–1963	7
1.3	Rivalry data (firms' annual reports)	13
1.4	Advertising rivalry results: one firm's generic reaction to the advertising outlay of its rivals	14
1.5	Sales and losses for borders, 1996–2009	15
1.6	Franchise rivalry results: one firm's generic reaction to the advertising outlay of its rivals	15
1.7	Companies' financials	17
2.1	Internet revenue and cost data	25
3.1	Long-term trends in the book publishing industry	52
3.2	Translog regression: nonseparable results, 1985–2002	57
3.3	Own elasticity by book categories estimated from regression results	59
3.4	Own elasticity and Lerner power index based on regression results	59
3A.1	US book stores (NAICS 451211) sales, 2000–current ($m)	62
3A.2	Time series data for the book publishing industry	63
3A.3	Historic trade trend data 1992–2006 ($ths.), paper and publishing products	64
3A.4	Hardback, paperback, and mass media prices	65
3A.5	Regression analysis of growth trends	66
3A.6	Book by book categories, 1985–2002 ($m)	71
3A.7	Revenues of book categories, 1985–2002: $m from Greco book	71

4.1	Productivity explained by wages, 1989–2007 BLS data	74
4.2	Industry total scale economy, 2004–2006	77
4.3	Production function book publishing industry sample, 1998–2007	78
4.4	Translog approximation of CES production function, BISG quantity, and compustat capital data	81
4A.1	Unemployment rate, nonagricultural private wage, and salary workers, publishing, except Internet: 2000–current	83
4A.2	Book publishers: NAICS 51113, average hourly earnings of production workers	83
4A.3	Industry technical data	84
4A.4	NAICS 511130, book publishers. Annual percentage change of industry productivity data, 1988–current	85
4A.5	Productivity, costs, and output indices, 1987–current	86
4A.6	Regression results for productivity on wages	86
4A.7	(Additional data) Regression results for productivity on wages	89
4A.8	Results use for translog/CES model of table T2-4 system	91
4A.9	GAMS model for the extraction of substitution parameters	92
5.1	Distribution aspects of book publishing	98
5.2	HHI calculation	98
5.3	Sales on concentration, SUR system estimates, 1963–2007 (available concentration data)	100
5.4	Size distribution of establishments, census data: 1992, 1997, 2002	102
5.5	Distribution of general, specialty, and college books, number of establishments by employees: 1997 versus 2002	103
5.6	Sales–employees distribution	104
6.1	Triad VAT and GST tax rates in percent	111
6.2	Historic rate trends ($ths dollars) in the PPI	112
6.3	CGE benefits due to improved allocation and policy mixes	114
6.4	PPI for major countries in the Triad regions	116
6.5	TAA certification and denial	118
6.6	Global computer market information and communication technology (ICT) spending	119
7.1	Five firms' share of toll revenues	125

Foreword

> One should prize above all possessions a field, a friend, and a book.
>
> Rav Hai Gaon, 11th century

Most economists have heard of Adam Smith's *Wealth of Nations*. (A few may even have read it.) The book, in two volumes, appeared in March 1776. After eight years of active work on the project, six at his home outside Edinburgh and then two more while living in London, Smith delivered the hard-copy manuscript to his publisher, William Strahan, sometime in the latter half of 1775. By early 1776, Strahan had printed either 500 or 750 copies (the historical record is unclear). They went on sale, at Strahan's shop in the Strand, on March 9. The book was an instant success, with five editions in English plus numerous foreign translations by the time Smith died just 14 years later. It has not stopped selling since.

Leaving aside the *Wealth of Nations*' postpublication success, the process just described is broadly familiar as the firsthand experience of many economists today, and countless other authors too, who wrote books published any time up to about 20 years ago. For more than two centuries following 1776, the routine of the book world remained little changed—just as it had for much of the two centuries before that. The process today is different. Most authors use an electronic word-processing system to produce their text, rather than writing it out longhand or dictating it to a secretary (as Smith reportedly did for parts of the *Wealth of Nations*). Most likewise submit the resulting product to their publishers in electronic rather than paper form.

The printers in turn use some similar electronic process to set the text. The often tedious matter of correcting set proofs and making other in-process revisions is likewise done electronically. Decisions on how many copies to print are different too; with today's technology the cost of printing additional copies, once the book is set, is so less that while there is little financial risk (other than storage) to printing too many copies, there is also little reason, apart from marketing considerations for a few hot-selling works, to bear it. The limiting cases of these technological changes in production are print-on-demand books, which an increasing number of publishers are doing, and self-publishing, which an increasing number of authors are doing.

The process of selling books, and buying them, is different too. Indeed, while the most significant changes to publishing and printing seem to be in place, at least for now, the activity of book buying and selling is only just in the immediacy of rapid evolution. Many bookstores still exist, some large and many more that are small. But increasingly readers look for books via the Internet, and many buy them that way too. In an interesting combination with important implications for the industry's future, some readers who visit their nearby bookstore to decide what to buy then turn to the Internet to buy it, so that the bookstore ends up providing a service for which it has no way of getting paid.

Finally, what it means to read, or have in one's possession, a "book" is changing as well. Electronic "readers"—the Kindle, the Nook, the Kobo, the ordinary iPad—have proliferated. Books are increasingly published in both physical and electronic form, and many of those that are not, including many books published long before anyone imagined the possibility of e-books, have been digitized. Someone who wants to consult a book but not necessarily read it need not even go to the library for a copy.

(A few years ago the *American Economic Review* published a paper of mine in which I referred to an essay, by the 17th-century French moralist Pierre Nicole, that first appeared in English in a volume published in London in 1695. The AER editor asked me to specify the pages in that volume for this particular essay. At first I feared this would be a long process; the Harvard library might not own a copy, and even if it did whoever controls such rarities probably wouldn't let me examine it anyway. I then thought to look for the book in the library's online catalog. Within five minutes I had downloaded the entire text, looked up the relevant page numbers and inserted them in the proofs the AER had sent me, and moved on to other matters.)

Lall Ramrattan and Michael Szenberg, in their insightful new book on *Revolutions in Book Publishing*, examine the economics of how books are produced and sold in just this context of sweeping technological change. Their work brings together a wide array of factual information—the volume is well worthwhile for the data it amasses alone—and serious economic analysis. Traditional industrial organization analysis, auction theory, search theory, game theory, and sophisticated econometric analysis are all parts of the toolkit they deploy.

As for economists everywhere, Ramrattan and Szenberg's starting place is to separate demand and supply—often trickier than it sounds, and no less so in the book business. In the bookselling industry, the distinction between price and nonprice competition, playing out in the competing worlds of brick-and-mortar bookstores and Internet marketing as well as of print books versus e-books, is of the essence in what they analyze. (Ramrattan and Szenberg conclude that the competition between print books and e-books is "a zero-sum game.") Moreover, as they clearly show, this competition has resulted in major changes not only in how books are bought and sold but also who is selling them; like many other industries, bookselling is undergoing major consolidation, and just in the past few years major firms like Borders and Crown Books have gone out of business. In their view, "Digitization lowers the marginal costs of firms, and tends to shift competition toward price collusion and into non-price areas such as service competition."

The focus of their analysis of the printing and publishing industry is likewise squarely on the effects of what they analyze as a consequence of massive "technological shocks." The implications—for economies of scale, for firms' pricing power and their financial returns, for the use of quality as a barrier to entry, for employment in the industry (which they show is declining, despite positive growth on just about all other industry measures)—are major. Interestingly, Ramrattan and Szenberg find that the elasticity of demand, in most sectors of the book industry (adult trade books, book clubs, elementary and high schools texts, mass market paperbacks, and the like) has been declining. Their explanation, in part, is that "the proliferation of electronic gadgets is a good and viable substitute for reading, so that people do not respond as before to a price cut." Changing technology is at the heart of their story.

What is also striking in Ramrattan and Szenberg's work is the combination of industry-level analysis with fine-grained detailed knowledge of the industry (really two interconnected industries: bookselling and printing and publishing) they are examining. The kind of industry-level analysis they carry out is, of course, the meat-and-potatoes stuff of the empirical economics of industrial organization. But who knew that Books-a-Million ships much of its inventory through its subsidiary, named American Wholesale? Or that American Wholesale has locations in Tuscumbia and Florence, Alabama? Ramrattan and Szenberg knew, and their detailed knowledge gives their industry-level analysis a depth and texture that is all too often missing in standard academic work.

People who write books also tend to read them. (Farmers also eat, and auto workers drive; but the relationship seems deeper for books.) Many economists will therefore find a special interest in this book, more so than in a similar work on some other industry. And plenty of noneconomists should find it of interest too; one does not have to be an economist to be interested in the economics of a product that is so central to personal pleasure, or human or professional development, or both. What Ramrattan and Szenberg have done here should find a broad audience. Anyone who reads it will learn from it.

Benjamin M. Friedman
Harvard University

Preface and Acknowledgments

Both of us possess a deep love affair with books that can be traced back to childhood. Lall's love of books began when one of his brothers, Suruj Rattan, died and bequeathed a small library of books to him. Those books became his teenage companions. In particular, Adam Smith's description of the pin factory drew clear pictures of his colonial experience of cane and rice processing, and ultimately steered Lall's career toward economics. Michael's love of books was stimulated even earlier in childhood, when his sister Esther taught him to read using the only book available to them—a biography of Felix Dzerzhinsky, the infamous head of the Cheka, the Soviet Security Service, after the Bolshevik Revolution. He read and reread the book numerous times during the last two years of the Second World War, while hiding from the Nazis in an attic with his immediate family. For Michael, this biography was a synthesis of fiction, poetry, and history that truly became a part of him.

The idea for this volume was conceived many years ago. The first publication by either of us on the book industry examined book consumption in the United States from 1952 to 1985. Since then, we have joined forces and continued to explore the evolution of the industry. The current state of the industry is an incredibly propitious time to publish a volume on book publishing, as it continues to undergo drastic changes whose long-term effects still remain to be seen.

To gain an adequate picture of this important industry, we utilized a variety of research methods. How right

Gustav Flaubert was when he observed that readers should not think that books dropped like meteorites from the sky! The principal objective of this study is to analyze, evaluate, and cast light on the changes in an industry where economics, commerce, technology, and culture intertwine.

While revising the manuscript, we reminded ourselves of Honore de Balzac, who was famous for his endless revisions, and also of Giuseppe Verdi, who was satisfied that he had written his opera scores perfectly the first time. If the analysis we present here provides a more realistic evaluation of the book industry, we feel that the effort has been worthwhile.

In the several years that have elapsed between the conception of this book and its publication, we amassed an enormous volume of debt. Our first vote of thanks must go to Ben Friedman, William Joseph Maier Professor of Political Economy and formerly Chairman of the Department of Economics at Harvard University, who extended to us many kindnesses in the past and agreed to pen the foreword to this volume. We know how lucky we are to have Mary Ellen Benedict, Chair of the Economics Department and Distinguished Professor at Bowling Green State University, as a treasured friend. She exemplifies the combination of effective leadership, humility, kindness, and cheerfulness. These are the things that really matter in life.

In 1656, Blaise Pascal observed: "I have made this letter longer than usual because I lack the time to make it short." In the same vein, George Stigler remarked that for many instructors, it takes five pages just to clear their throat. We are grateful to the individuals who helped us get to the heart of the matter and make this a stronger book.

At Palgrave Macmillan, Stacy Noto has been a model editor; we are most grateful for her assistance in shaping and refining the manuscript and expertly shepherding this volume to completion.

We are particularly indebted to Leah Pollack for her superb editorial assistance. She revised the manuscript with flawless accuracy and timeliness, moving it cheerfully and steadily toward publication.

We feel an immeasurable debt of gratitude toward Victor Fuchs, the Henry J. Kaiser, Jr., Professor at Stanford University, emeritus, for his steadfast support and encouragement that have spanned more than four decades. We also wish to acknowledge Vernon Smith, the 2002 Nobel Prize winner, who graciously penned the foreword to our recent volume *Economic Ironies Throughout History* and is a major contributor to our work-in-progress *Intellectual Collaborative Experiences*.

Others whose aid over the years we are pleased to acknowledge include the members of the Executive Board of Omicron Delta Epsilon—the Honor Society in Economics—for being an important source of inspiration, encouragement, and support; Professors Mary Ellen Benedict, Alan Grant, Paul W. Grimes, Stacey Jones, Katherine A. Nantz, Farhang Niroomand, Robert Rycroft, Joseph M. Santos, Ali Zadeh, and the Coordinator of the ODE Central Office, Phyllis Carter. We are grateful for their collegiality and deep friendship. We are particularly indebted to Farhang Niroomand, Dean, University of Houston-Victoria, for his wise advice on various matters over the years.

I owe an awesome debt of gratitude to two extraordinary individual—Iuliana Ismailescu and Oscar Camargo—for their goodness of heart, enduring support, positive attitude, gracious good cheer, and deep friendship. In the same category, I would like to include Anna Geller, who is an outstanding marketing professor. They are a constant source of affection. I also want to recognize Elki and Chaim Herzog, Batya, Chanoch and Ephraim Kunin, Devora and Nachum Wolmark, and Ayala Szenberg. They did the work with diligence, character, good humor, exactitude, and patience. They all have lightened many a task. Their assistance was incalculable and I am grateful to them.

My heart still warms with gratitude toward Sadia Nabi, who recently assumed a prominent position with the International Fund for Agricultural Development in Rome. She, along with my other past talented and devoted graduate research assistants Ester Robbins Budek, Leo Faleev, Lisa Ferraro, Laura Garcia, Hema Gejaraj, Yelena Glantz, Janet Lieben-Ulman, Jennifer Loftus, Andrea Pascarelli, Joshua Schenkein, Sandra Shpilberg, Marina Slavina, Janet Ulman, Aleena Wee, and Lisa Youel, helped directly and indirectly in more ways than I can list to make this book the offspring of our partnership. Their input lives on in these pages.

We acknowledge the contribution of Anna Geller, Iva Juric, and Aaron Ross, who are imbued with unremitting kindness and exactitude. In addition, a number of former students deserve thanks for their invaluable input and assistance: Frank DiMeglio, Lorene Hiris, Richard Larocca, Cathyann Tully, and Alan Zimmerman. They all occupy high educational and administrative positions at various universities.

Also, thanks to the many who have in their own special ways supported my efforts. They include Richard Baker, Cindy Dumas—Administrative Operations Coordinator, Economic Science Institute, Chapman University, Larisa Parkhomovskaya, Nicola Simpson, and Justyna Tuniewicz.

Thanks to Renee Blinder, Coordinator of Advisement and Counseling at Touro, and to Josh Zilberberg for their genuine warmth, support, and wise guidance. We also wish to mention Naomi Broker, who is pursuing her doctorate in physical therapy at Hunter College: here we find that rare combination of scholarship, character, and beauty that dwell together.

Once more, thanks to Naomi, my daughter, an ophthalmologist, and to my son, Avi, a lawyer. They are my fortitude; I can always count on them when I need someone to lean on. They are indispensable to our family—a true blessing.

Special thanks to Touro's vice presidents Stanley Boylan, Robert Goldschmidt, Moshe Krupka, and Deans Henry Abramson, Barry Bressler, Sandra Brock, Moshe Sokol, and Marian Stoltz-Loike for their ongoing support and commitment to our scholarly endeavors.

My deepest gratitude goes to Dr. Alan Kadish, president of Touro College and University System, for his extraordinary leadership, dedication to excellence, kindness, cheerfulness, and inspiration. Without his generosity and encouragement, this volume would not have been possible. He holds the wheel and steers Touro's ship in the right direction.

palgrave▸pivot

www.palgrave.com/pivot

1
General Introduction

Abstract: *The book industry has been marked by four distinct phases of technological advances: the Civil War period, World War I, World War II, and the modern period of high-tech development. Today, bookstores are dwindling and the Internet is the preferred marketplace for both buyers and sellers. Consumers are increasingly reading books in digitized form on electronic devices. Feedbacks in the old Structure, Conduct, and Performance paradigm have made predictions difficult in the industry. We apply methods of analysis that view industry players' rivalry behavior in a gaming setting, taking a new perspective on price and nonprice competition that also encompasses bidding, advertising and R&D expenditures that have become important dimensions of the market order of the industry.*

Ramrattan, Lall, and Michael Szenberg. *Revolutions in Book Publishing: The Effects of Digital Innovation on the Industry.* New York: Palgrave Macmillan, 2016. DOI: 10.1057/9781137576217.0006.

Not since Gutenberg printed his first Bible has the book industry undergone such rapid and widespread change. Digital technology has revolutionized the industry and expanded the very definition of what makes a book. Paper books, e-books, self-publishing, books promoted by social media and uploaded straight to our Kindles: all are viable options in publishing's brave new world.

Why is there a need for a study of the book industry? First, in the industrial organization literature, the study of the book industry is conspicuously absent. Walter Adams and James Brock's *The Structure of American Industry*, now in its 12th edition, has never covered the book industry. There are other publications that have studied aspects of the industry, including Greco's 2005 book and Canoy's 2005 entry in the *Handbook of the Economics of Art and Culture*, but they are generally light on analysis and research. Specialized institutions and industry groups such as Bowker and the Book Industry Study Group (BISG) continuously publish opinion pieces on the industry outlook in blog posts and press releases, but these are not comprehensive.

Second, it is important to keep track of the technological shocks to the industry, which have already had both drastic and incremental effects (Helpman, 1998, p. 2). The most radical changes to the industry have been in the areas of digital media and communication, while more incremental changes are continuously appearing as firms create, adopt, and apply new technologies. The data that drive the book industry are often sparse. We have worked to fill a gap in the existing literature by collecting and analyzing the available data with statistical techniques, reconciling them in a way that brings coherence to the data and provides insight through the lenses of traditional economic models.

While the new, digitalized market paradigm does not quite usurp the traditional brick-and-mortar approach to bookselling, traditional bookstores are in a survival-of-the-fittest mode of competition within the Internet domain. The market for e-books is not in a win-win relation with the market for print books; if anything, they are in a zero-sum game relation where the increased share of e-books is gained at the expense of print books' market share.

We see the book industry as competing in two layers: bookstores and the Internet. The traditional weapons of competition, such as pricing, advertising, and number of stores, are still significant strategies—but nonprice competition has been particularly elevated. Digital technology has revolutionized the ways of the industry with regard to both supply and demand.

Only time will tell whether the book industry will continue to march on in a recognizable form, with brick-and-mortar bookstores selling books you can hold in your hands. Through empirical analysis, this book will document the changes that have wrought such intense transformation on the industry and brought it to its current, critical point.

Outline of chapters

Introduction: Transformation of the industry

The book industry has been marked by four distinct phases of technological advances: the Civil War period, World War I, World War II, and the modern period of high-tech development. Today, bookstores are dwindling and the Internet is the preferred marketplace for both buyers and sellers. Consumers are increasingly reading books in digitized form on electronic devices. Feedbacks in the old Structure, Conduct, and Performance paradigm have made predictions difficult in the industry. We apply methods of analysis that view industry players' rivalry behavior in a gaming setting, taking a new perspective on price and nonprice competition that also encompasses bidding, advertising, and R&D expenditures that have become important dimensions of the market order of the industry.

Chapter 2: The blades of supply and demand and technology

When supply is drastically modified by new technology, it takes on a dimension of shock, resulting in models that contain incomplete information content and more challenging exogenous and endogenous phenomena. We identify new demand parameters for the industry. Consumers can now comparison-shop for bargains and choose between different ways to read books and allocate their time. These options determine their consumption and human capital formation. While technological advances in this industry are now at the General Purpose level, their role still seems unsettled. Advancement in the book industry is of the modern endogenous growth type associated with increasing returns as capital accumulates. The resulting competitive behavior between firms adheres to discriminating pricing in an imperfect market structure within the new global technological environment.

Chapter 3: Consumption drives the industry

Consumption is a driver of the book industry, and therefore impacts profits as the state of the economy changes. The overall state is that production rates are almost twice as large as consumption rates—but prices remain high, partly because they are traditionally cost-push in nature. The highest-cost aspects of the industry have traditionally been paper, platemaking, printing, binding, and book returns. Information technology is changing those costs as book production moves online or overseas. As a result, the industry has experienced some severe short-term business cycles that have been devastating to firms like Borders Books, which exited the industry in 2011. Our empirical study shows that price is elastic for all major book categories, indicating that price competition is still alive, though the industry also practices nonprice competition.

Chapter 4: Production is in a transitional mode

Production aspects of the book industry are in a state of perpetual mobility, with printed books facing strong competition from virtual space, Print on Demand (PoD), and e-books technologies. Our empirical analysis attempts to reconcile contrary views about increasing and constant returns to scale, using generally available data and standard econometric techniques. We embrace both the simple Cobb-Douglas and CES models of production. The Cobb-Douglas model indicates constant returns with weak statistical results, while the CES model indicates increasing returns. The overall results are subject to wide interpretation, underscoring a monopolistic structure, or a bilateral monopolistic model. The results also have an impact on the modern discussion of increasing returns, which is normally sourced to the socialization of modern technological advances.

Chapter 5: Distribution

Distribution channels for books have evolved from small bookstores, to larger superstores, to the more impersonal Internet. Larger bookstores seem to have a dominant position in these activities through mergers and cooperations, yet this does not show up as high concentration for the industry. On the average, the concentration seems to be held in check from cooperation with smaller independent firms for the purpose of reaching customers in the suburbs or as independent suppliers on the Internet. Nevertheless, sales remain responsive to concentration, which in turn is responsive to mergers and an index of market power. Some modern distribution problems are also related to inventory management.

Chapter 6: Printing and publishing in international competition

International competition requires the estimates of consumer, producer, and welfare optimum in a general equilibrium framework to account for how agents make substitution within countries. The world flow of GDP and FDI concentrates among the three regions of North America, Europe, and Asia. Our analysis proceeds with an eye for free trade according to the classical hypothesis, and a preference for domestic adjustment according to the Keynesian hypothesis for these regions. North America and Europe did much better under the classical than under the Keynesian hypothesis. Some countries, such as China and India in Asia, the United Kingdom, France, and Germany in Europe; and the United States in North America are spotlighted for more extended analysis.

Chapter 7: Internet technology and the book

Books possess inherent characteristics that make them a natural product to buy and sell online. They are easy to ship, inexpensive to warehouse and inventory, easy to review and rate, can be test read, and can easily be searched. The Internet provides a widened audience with low-cost, 24-hour access to a diverse world of selections. The Internet is the battlefield at the conjunction of production, consumption, and distribution, and has become more and more competitive for book publishers. The Internet has made value chains more efficient, particularly in the area of digitized books, where digital information is available to intermediaries who produce books from the digital copies. Accounting records are kept of various sales transactions by region, creating a source of information economies.

History and definition of the book industry

Historically speaking, the book publishing industry has undergone four landmark waves, the results of new and evolving technologies. The Civil War period saw the first major boost to book publishing, as industrial activities began to dominate agriculture, giving rise to informational books that explained various industries. World War I spurred the invention of radio communication, aviation, and photography, creating another wave of publications for interested readers. World War II witnessed a proliferation of how-to books, addressing the needs of a large population of unskilled laborers who were called to task. The modern wave gets its boost from the advent and constant evolution of the Information Technology field.

During the 1960s, publishing houses in the United States began to merge to a concentration level. In the 1970s, 15 companies dominated the industry, and by the 1990s, only 7 remained, mainly through conglomerate mergers that spread over media and motion pictures. The dominant book companies included the Borders Group, Barnes & Noble, Books-a-Million, and Amazon.com.

The book industry faces an array of problems encountered by modern industries that stem from the tide of technology and globalization. Old problems such as mergers and pricing, along with new problems such as copyright piracy and outsourcing, top the agenda. Technology has produced gadgets and games that compete for readers' time. Foreign publishing outfits can now produce books just as well as US publishers. Yet the book industry is still growing, albeit at a modest pace.

The book industry is very diverse. On the publication side, in 2002 the North American Industry Classification System (NAICS) classified Book Publishers under the code NAICS 511130. Industry code 516110 covers Internet Publishing and Broadcasting; industry code 323110 covers Printing books without publishing; industry code 512230 covers Music Publishers; and industry code 454390 covers Other Direct Selling Establishments. These new classifications overtake the Standard Industrial Classification (SIC) codes 2731 and 2741. Magazine and periodical publishers are covered under NAICS 511120, which overlaps with SIC 2741 of the book publishing industry, and exclusively deals with SIC 2721. This category includes establishments primarily engaged in publishing, or in publishing and printing, books and pamphlets. Establishments primarily engaged in printing or in printing and binding (but not publishing) books and pamphlets are classified in SIC 2732: Book Printing.

On the sales side, NAICS 4512111 includes General Bookstores. NAICS 4512112 covers Specialty Bookstores, which include reference, religious, and professional books. NAICS 4512113 covers College Bookstores.

The general inefficiency in the reporting of data translates into difficulties in defining the industry. As a result, we outline the scope of data coverage by major providers for comparison and use in this text. Table 1.1 displays these categories for the major data providers.

Growth trends

A few studies have looked at the Book Publishing industry from a long-term perspective. Studying book publishing as a subcategory of the Retail industry, David Schwartzman (1971) found that the book publishing industry declined over time. Employment grew slowly, from a quarter of a percent annually from 1929 to 1958, to approximately 1 percent annually from 1958 to 1963, as indicated in Table 1.2.

Another long-term perspective is the output of books. Jean Peters tabulated the numbers of books produced every decade from 1980 to

TABLE 1.1 *Industry classification*

	Statistical abstract of the United States	Census: book sales	BLS series data	BISG
Revenues				
Quantities	NAICS 51113			
Sales		NAICS 451211		NAICS 51113
Employment			NAICS 51113	
Capital	SIC 2731 (1987–1997)			
Inventory	NAICS 51113 (1998–2006)			

TABLE 1.2 *Long-term growth, 1929–1963*

	Retail industry				Book industry			
	Total Retail Sales ($m)	Annual Pct. Change (Simple)	Cur. $ Sales ($m)	Annual Pct. Change (Simple)	Const. $ Sales (1957–1959$)	Annual Pct. Change (Simple)	Emp. (Ths.)	Annual Pct. Change (Simple)
1929	47,769.6		117		195.1		15.3	
1958	194,268.9	10.58%	282.4	4.87%	282.5	1.54%	16.4	0.25%
1963	238,695.9	4.57%	395.3	8.00%	379.5	6.87%	17.1	0.85%

Source: Compiled from David Schwartzman (1971). Data Appendixes.

1990. Only two decades showed negative growth: −26.78 percent in 1920–1929 and −7.07 percent in 1940–1949 (Peters, 1992, p. 18). Overall, steady growth is the dominant characteristic for this industry.

Methodology

The method we employ is empirical in nature. First, industry analysis deals with data analysis. We will gather appropriate time series and cross-section data and perform economic analysis. The data that drives the book industry is often sparse, and the task of collecting and analyzing is with statistical techniques is filling in a gap in the literature. One challenge is to locate these sparse and dispersed data that are in the hands of the government and private sectors, and reconcile them in a way that brings coherence to the data and insight through the lenses of traditional economic models.

The old approach to industry study must now be flexed to accommodate the influences of the digital world. The demand and supply aspects of the market are now layered into brick-and-mortar stores and online activities. While we see the effects of technology—the most important supply side variable—everywhere in the book industry, an old story pointed out long ago that a technology must address many niches in demand (Helpman, 1998, p. 33). Some of those demand niches will be filled by old technology, while others will be inadequately filled. As the technology becomes general purpose in nature, new demand will arise.

The demand and supply approach will lead to the consideration of the production, consumption, and distribution sides of the industry. Production has acquired a digital boost, allowing books to be printed on demand, substantially lowering marginal costs. Consumption now involves an Internet search procedure that's much enabled by search engines and seller web sites. On the distribution side, Amazon.com has taught traditional booksellers how to sell without bookstores.

The traditional approach to industry study that seeks causal relationship between an industry's Structure, Conduct and Performance (SPC) is now in oblivion. The paradigm had too many feedbacks to be useful for predictive purposes. Traditionally, the SCP model predicts conduct from structure, and then performance from conduct. That causal way of reasoning is not watertight, but rather is characterized by feedbacks. For example, in filling a glass of water, we use our eyes to decide when to turn the faucet off. Similarly, our beliefs about market structure can change with observation of changes in a firm's behavior or performance. Thus, structure can be dependent on either conduct or performance, and both structure and conduct can be modified by government policies, which follow from conduct.

Now in vogue are case studies and gaming insights showing how one company reacts to its rivals. Firms are inclined to make the first move, as in the case of e-books and e-readers. Others tend to follow or ignore. Before its demise, Borders books employed a diversification strategy to sell nonbook items of an educational nature, including toys and games, to stem the tide of e-book competition (Bowker Annual Report, 2011, p. 252). Unfortunately, the company did not survive.

Background of major players in the industry

Amazon.com

Until recently, the structure of the online book industry in the United States was concentrated in the hands of a few firms—Amazon.com, Barnes & Noble, Borders, and Books-a-Million Inc.—and shrank even further when borders were eroded in February 2011. Amazon.com opened as "Earth's Biggest Bookstore" in July 1995, and later expanded into other product groups such as apparel, jewelry, computers, and movies. Amazon is a worldwide venture, operating under www.amazon.com (United States), www.amazon.co.uk (United Kingdom), www.amazon.de (Germany), www.amazon.fr (France), www.amazon.co.jp (Japan), www.amazon.ca (Canada), www.amazon.cn (China), www.joyo.cn, www.shopbop.com, and www.endless.com. Amazon also designs, manufactures, and sells a wireless e-reading device, the Amazon Kindle. It focuses on low prices and convenience in shopping.

Through its Amazon Merchant and Amazon Marketplace programs, Amazon created a colossal window for others to sell merchandise through their website. Amazon charges a fixed fee, sales commissions, and/or per-unit activity fees. In 2008, approximately 53 percent of Amazon's net sales occurred in North America, and the rest were international. In 2008, media products accounted for 58 percent of net sales, electronics, and other general merchandise 39 percent, and other products 3 percent.

Barnes & Noble

Barnes & Noble, a traditional brick-and-mortar bookstore, expanded on the Internet through several significant moves. On November 12, 1998, Bertelsmann AG, a publishing company operating Doubleday, Random House, and other publishers, acquired 50 percent interest in its online venture. On March 18, 1999, Barnes & Noble offered 20 percent of its share to the public under NASDAQ (BNBN), and used the proceeds mostly to enhance its online operations (Annual Report, 1998). In 2001, Barnes & Noble acquired SparkNotes.com, a website specializing in study aids. In 2003, Barnes & Noble purchased a 60-year-old company, Sterling Publishing, which specialized in nonfiction books.

As of January 31, 2009, Barnes & Noble was the largest bookseller in the United States, with 778 bookstores. In the 1980s, it experimented with online sales through Trintex as a joint venture with Sears and IBM. In the 1990s, it sold books through CompuServe. Barnes & Noble's major online venture started with America Online in March 1997, with the launching of Barnes & Noble.com (Annual Report, 1997, p. 4). The company's Annual Report that year boasted: "In 1997, over 250,000 customers in 149 countries purchased their books from our online store. The availability of every book in print combined with deep discounts and fast delivery has made BarnesandNoble.com the online global bookseller of choice" (ibid., p. 9).

Borders

In 1971, Tom and Louis Borders opened the Borders Book Shop in Ann Arbor, MI. In 1992, the Borders-Walden Group was formed, which included an earlier purchase of Brentano by Walden. In 1995, a public corporation was formed under the name Borders Group, Inc. In 2001, the group offered online shopping through Amazon.com. Borders Group maintained several overseas outposts in the United Kingdom and Malaysia, along with its 515 superstores in the United States.

Borders met strong competition from Amazon and Barnes & Noble in the e-book market. The company's sales of print books suffered from the strong competition in e-books (Bowker Annual Report, 2011, p. 452). From 1998 to 2009, its sales per square foot fell by approximately 50 percent, even as the company had doubled the number of its super stores from 256 to 511. Borders was forced into bankruptcy in 2011.

Books-a-Million

Books-a-Million was incorporated in Delaware in September 1992. It was a merger with ARS Group, Inc. (ARS), which in turn was a merger of Bookland Stores, Inc., and Hibbett Sporting Goods, Inc., formed in 1991 and 1994, respectively. Books-a-Million sells books and other items through its chain of retail bookstores and on the Internet. It is a subsidiary of American Wholesale Book Company, Inc., Booksamillion.com, Inc., and BAM Card Services.

The company operates in both the retail and Internet segments of the book market. Its recent strategy was opportunistic, namely, by backfilling markets in states such as Maine and South Dakota, where Borders stores had closed. As of January 2012, the company operated 204 superstores, and had been selling the Nook digital device since 2011 (Bowker Annual Report, 2011, p. 452; Annual Report, 2012).

Rival behavior

Traditional theory expects some rivalry in advertising expenditures, number of bookstores, R&D expenditures, price, and services. We explore rivalrous behavior from a symmetric hypothesis:

> **Hypothesis: [Symmetry]:** *Firms within the book industry look at their nonprice rivals symmetrically.*

This hypothesis can be approached in several steps. First, we select the dependent variable, say Advertising: in the case of advertising rivalry for a particular firm, say Amazon. Second, we postulate that Amazon will react to the previous period's advertising of the other firms: Barnes & Noble, Books-a-Million, and Borders. Third, we assume that Amazon's ability to react depends on its current liquidity situation, as measured by its cash flow or sales.

Model and specification

Other rivalrous variables may be added to the independent variable set. For instance, firms that have stores, such as Barnes & Noble, Books-a-Million, and Borders, may also be in competition with regard to the number of stores they have each period. Amazon does not sell through stores, and therefore will not have this variable in its specification. A generic specification for firm can then be written as follows:

$$AD\,of\,Firm_{i,t} = f(AD\,of\,Firm_{j,t-1}, CF\,of\,Firm_{i,t}, Stores_{i,t}, R\,\&\,D_{i,t})$$

In this equation, AD is advertising expenditures; CF is cash flow, which is measured as net income plus depreciation; stores are the number of stores existing for the firm; and R&D is research and development expenditures. The rivalry will be between the ith and jth firm, and t is current time period. By switching the place of the dependent variable with either Stores or R&D, one gets a rivalry model in those variables.

In this overview, we start our competitive analysis of the book industry by estimating the symmetry hypothesis for advertising and stores. The specification is in logarithmic form so that the coefficient will measure elasticity of responsiveness of one firm's outlay to the other. A priori, we expect that all the coefficients will be positive. A firm will react positively to a rival outlay of advertising, number of stores, or R&D expenditures for fear that it might lose market share if it does not react.

Estimating the model

Table 1.3 displays the data we gathered from the firm's 10k and Annual Report for the purpose of examining the symmetric completion in the industry. Each company states its reporting date in the annual report. Table 1.3 shows the data associated with the year the report specifies. Amazon's advertising and promotional costs consist primarily of online advertising (Annual Report, 2006, p. 56). Barnes & Noble combines its advertising and administrative costs under the heading of advertising (Annual Report, 2010, p. 36).

Regarding the stores variable, this can be thought of as franchise, number of stores, or operational rivalry. A book company's growth may be explained by the number of stores it owns, that is, net of new additions and losses. Firms such as Barnes & Noble and Books-a-Million distinguish rivalry between the number of superstores and regular stores they own. The rate of this type of rivalrous expansion depends on a number of important factors for the firms, including the state of consumer confidence, availability of locations and personnel, lease terms, liquidity

TABLE 1.3 *Rivalry data (firms' annual reports)*

	Advertising expenditures ($m)				Number of stores			Sales ($m)			
Year	AMZ	B&N	BOR	BAM	BAM	B&M	BOR	AMZ	BAM	B&M	BOR
1990	NA	183	NA	12	NA	NA	NA	NA	65	NA	880
1991	NA	195	NA	13	NA	NA	NA	NA	73	NA	921
1992	NA	221	NA	17	NA	NA	NA	NA	95	NA	1087
1993	NA	263	244	22	NA	NA	NA	NA	123	1184	1337
1994	NA	311	281	32	124	966	NA	NA	172	1371	1623
1995	NA	377	333	44	129	997	NA	1	230	1511	1977
1996	6	456	375	51	151	1008	158	16	279	1749	2448
1997	39	540	410	59	165	1011	204	148	325	1959	2797
1998	133	577	485	66	173	1009	256	610	348	2266	3006
1999	176	651	558	80	180	1468	300	1640	404	2595	3486
2000	180	813	674	85	185	1886	349	2762	419	2999	4376
2001	138	904	736	92	204	1934	385	3122	443	3271	4870
2002	114	965	745	94	207	886	434	3933	443	3388	5269
2003	109	1125	745	95	202	842	482	5264	460	3486	5951
2004	141	1052	820	99	206	820	504	6921	475	3699	4874
2005	168	1134	871	109	205	779	528	8490	504	3880	5103
2006	226	1202	952	113	206	793	567	10711	520	4031	5287
2007	306	1250	988	117	208	798	541	14835	535	4064	5411
2008	420	1252	956	117	220	778	518	19166	513	3775	5122
2009	680	1392	840	115	223	777	511	24509	509	3242	5808
2010	1029	1629	711	118	231	1357	489	34204	495	2791	6999
2011	1630	1739	589	120	211	1341	NA	48077	469	2253	7129

Note: AMS: Amazon; BOR: Borders; and BAM: Books-a-Million.
Source: Firms' Annual Reports.

constraints, and firms' cash flow, and could require a further breakout of equation for these items (Books-a-Million Annual Report, 2012, p. 12).

A special case of the estimating procedure is to restrict the coefficients of the predictor rivalry variable. Amazon, for instance, will be reacting to the advertising of Barnes & Noble, Books-a-Million, and Borders. The restriction in that case is to make the coefficient of three firms the same. In other words, rather than investigating how Amazon reacts to the three forms individually, we estimate one coefficient for the reaction of all three of Amazon's rivals.

Other relevant concerns for the estimated technique include selecting a proper method of estimation. We opted for Three Stage Least square, a method that integrates the correlation of errors among firms belonging to the same industry. Proper account is taken for serial correlation as well, using auto regressive procedures.

In estimating the model, we substituted sales for cash flow because many years of the cash flow data are negative, and since the model is logarithmic in fit, we cannot take the log of a negative number.

Results of advertising rivalry hypothesis

The results of Table 1.4 indicate that all the advertising coefficients are positive and significant at the 99 percent level. Amazon reacts the most, with elasticity 0.37, to its other three rivals in advertising competition. Barnes & Noble is the next largest reactor, with an elasticity of 0.22. Borders and Books-a-Million are by far smaller reactors, with elasticity of 0.01 and 0.04, respectively.

The supporting variables in the regression do not perform strongly. While significant, the Borders sales coefficient and Barnes & Noble Stores coefficient display negative signs.

Results of franchising rivalry hypothesis

We have made an examination of franchise rivalry that is similar to advertising rivalry. In this case, Amazon, which does not compete with regard to the number of bookstores, leaves franchise rivalry to Barnes & Noble, Books-a-Million, and Borders. We used similar techniques for the

TABLE 1.4 *Advertising rivalry results: one firm's generic reaction to the advertising outlay of its rivals*

Estimates	Amazon	Barnes & Noble	Borders	Book-a-Month
Constant	−19.65	5.64	4.05	−3.88
t-values	(8.38)***	(3.36)***	(20.95)***	(4.26)***
3 Firms AD	0.37	0.22	0.01	0.04
t-values	(3.18)***	(9.85)***	(2.66)***	(4.32)***
Sales	0.47	−0.11	−0.44	1.04
t-values	(74.59)***	(0.67)	−(12.37)***	(14.20)***
Stores		−0.19	1.01	0.24
t-values		(2.95)***	(36.27)***	1.64
ADJ R-Sq.	97.85	86.72	95.9	98.9
Observ.	13	12	12	12

Note: *** = 99%, ** = 95%, and * = 90 significance levels.

TABLE 1.5 Sales and losses (in gray) for borders, 1996–2009

1996	1997	1998	1999	2000	2001	2002	2003	2004	2005	2006	2007	2008	2009
158	204	256	300	349	385	434	482	504	528	567	541	518	511
$259	$261	$256	$255	$255	$245	$237	$223	$227	$232	$236	$228	$203	$173

TABLE 1.6 Franchise rivalry results: one firm's generic reaction to the advertising outlay of its rivals

Estimates	Barnes & Noble	Borders	Books-a-Million
Const.	16.22	−4.03	3.02
t-values	11.90***	26.44*	7.22***
2 Firms Stores	1.13	0.04	0.04
t-values	1.81***	3.36***	3.63
Sales	−1.57	−0.37	0.01
t-values	5.10***	8.23***	0.22
Advertising	1.38	0.97	0.34
t-values	2.23***	23.57***	4.02
ADJ R-Sq.	0.81	0.98	77.6
Observ.	12	12	12

estimation of franchise rivalry as we did for advertising rivalry. Table 1.6 shows that the firms do engage in franchise rivalry in a symmetric manner. Barnes & Noble reacts the most, with elasticity of 1.13, and the other two firms react similarly with an elasticity of 0.04.

In franchise rivalry, advertising expenditure lends positive support to the number of franchises, except for the case of Books-a-Million, for which the coefficient was not significant.

The sales variable requires some additional information. *A priori* we learned from Borders' bankruptcy case that as new stores were created, sales fell consistently. Court records indicate that for the years 1996–2009, Borders lost an average of $235 per year per square foot of store space.

We use the sales data to make a restriction on Borders' sales coefficient to be negative to reflect that observation. The results of the sales estimates show negative relations between the number of stores and sales for Barnes & Noble and Borders. The sales coefficient for BAM is not significant.

Results of R & D rivalry hypothesis

One should also assess technological rivalry among firms. Ideally, a set of expenditures on technological development should have been

16   *Revolutions in Book Publishing*

collected for the data set in Table 1.1. Lacking that data, one cannot make a statistical model for R&D rivalry. Only Amazon.com provides R&D data, reporting those expenditures under "technology and content" data, which involves investment in "seller platforms, web services, digital initiatives, and expansion of new and existing product categories, as well as in technology infrastructure to enhance the customer experience, improve our process efficiencies and support our infrastructure web services." (Annual Report, 2007, p. 23).

Figure 1.1 shows the plot of Amazon's versus NAICS 511, publishing, and R&D expenditures for 1998–2007. Amazon's data is from various 10k/annual reports. NAICS data is from the National Science Foundation (http://www.nsf.gov/statistics/srvyrdexpenditures/). While the trend is decidedly upward, Amazon's share of the publishing industry data is small, amounting to only about 3 percent in the later years. The first implication is that the share of R&D is perhaps spread among many other companies. But as far as customer experience goes, restricted to e-readers, a few companies are dominant: specifically, Amazon with its Kindle and Barnes & Noble with its Nook, which has about a third of the market share in e-readers.

For a more recent view of the companies under study, Table 1.7 shows the financial condition of the major Internet companies. Internet sales alone are not broken out. Except for the Borders Group, which performed poorly during the Great Recession, the other companies show positive current returns. While Borders' cash flow (Net income + Depreciation) was positive in 2008, it was negative for the first half of 2009. Borders was the only company that experienced negative net income during the recession, a strong signal that disaster was underway.

The Internet firms strive for perpetual innovation in Internet retailing. By fostering independent merchants, expansion into broader product groups, and low shipping, Amazon was able to stem the tide of the recent recession (Business Week Art).

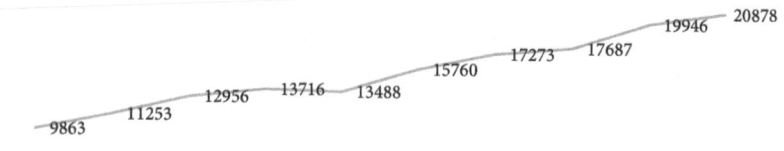

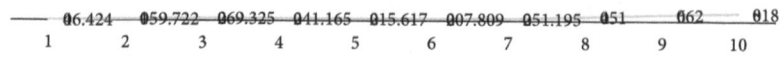

FIGURE 1.1   *Amazon versus Naics 511 R&D, 1998–2007 ($m)*

TABLE 1.7 *Companies' financials ($m & %)*

Year	Net Inc.	Depr.	Revs.	% Ret. on equity	Cap. Exp.	% Ret. on assets
Barnes & Noble (year ending January)						
2004	152	167	5,951	13.3	163	4.7
2005	123	184	4,874	10.3	185	3.5
2006	147	174	5,103	12.9	187	4.5
2007	151	170	5,261	13.2	179	4.7
2008	136	172	5,411	12.1	197	4.2
2009	85.4	174	5,122	8.6	193	2.7
2010	36.7	209	5811	4.0	128	1.1
2011	-74	229	6999	NA	110	NA
2012	-68.9	238	7129	NA	164	NA
Amazon (year ending December)						
2003	353	783	5,264	NA	46	1.7
2004	588	75.7	6,921	NA	891	21.8
2005	333	121	8,490	NA	204	9.6
2006	190	205	10,711	56.1	216	4.7
2007	476	271	14,835	58.5	224	8.8
2008	645	340	19,166	33.3	333	8.7
2009	902	206	24,509	22.8	373	8.2
2010	152	568	34,204	19.0	979	7.1
2011	631	1182	48,077	80.6	1811	2.9
Borders Group (filed bankruptcy in 2011) (year ending January)						
2000	90.3				144.7	
2001	73.8				138.7	
2002	87.4				90.7	
2003	111.7		3,513.0		121.5	
2004	120.0	104	3,731.0	11.2	100.5	5.2
2005	131.9	112.9	3,903.0	12	115.5	5.1
2006	101.0	121.5	4,079.2	10	196.3	3.9
2007	−151.3	130.0	4,113.5	NA	204.2	NA
2008	−157.4	109.9	3,820.9	NA	142.7	NA
2009	−186.7	107.1	3,275.4	NA	79.9	NA
2010	−109.4	98.8	2,823.9	NA	17.9	NA
2011	−299.0	77.8	2,274.9	NA	18.1	NA
Books-a-Million (year ending January)						
2000	5.9	13.8	404.1		13.5	
2001	3.1	14.8	418.6		12.4	
2002	4.0	15.6	442.9		11.7	
2003	1.4	16.3	442.7		17.1	
2004	7.2	15.7	460.2		9.1	
2005	10.2	17.8	475.2		14.9	
2006	13.1	15.6	503.8		11.3	
2007	18.9	14.1	520.4	12.5	16.2	6.1
2008	16.5	14.0	535.1	12.9	16.9	5.6
2009	10.6	14.4	513.3	10.4	19.8	3.8
2010	13.8	14.4	508.4	12.6	10.7	5.0
2011	9.4	15.3	495.0		16.8	
2012	−2.8	16.6	468.5		24.3	

Source: NetAdvantage—FTXT & Mergent Data Bases.

2
Overview of Price and Nonprice Competition

Abstract: *When supply is drastically modified by new technology, it takes on a dimension of shock, resulting in models that contain incomplete information content and more challenging exogenous and endogenous phenomena. We identify new demand parameters for the industry. Consumers can now comparison-shop for bargains and choose between different ways to read books and allocate their time. These options determine their consumption and human capital formation. While technological advances in this industry are now at the General Purpose level, their role still seems unsettled. Advancement in the book industry is of the modern endogenous growth type associated with increasing returns as capital accumulates. The resulting competitive behavior between firms adheres to discriminating pricing in an imperfect market structure within the new global technological environment.*

Ramrattan, Lall, and Michael Szenberg. *Revolutions in Book Publishing: The Effects of Digital Innovation on the Industry.* New York: Palgrave Macmillan, 2016.
DOI: 10.1057/9781137576217.0007

Overview of Price and Nonprice Competition 19

Investigation of price competition in the online industry takes the form of price dispersion. Analysts test for nondifference between the online and conventional sellers. Empirically, analysts investigate how potential consumers conduct book searches on the web in order to get the lowest price.

Pricing of books on the Internet has a story to tell about the structure of the book publishing industry. An old version of the story tells us that if firms price their products similarly, then some suggestion of collusion in pricing is involved. A more modern version is that prices are dispersed, and the consumer searches until the marginal cost of an additional search exceeds the marginal benefits.

In this section, we will refer to Figure 2.1, which suggests how prices are determined in the industry. Figure 2.1 contains two main columns dealing with price and nonprice competition. Other links to the two

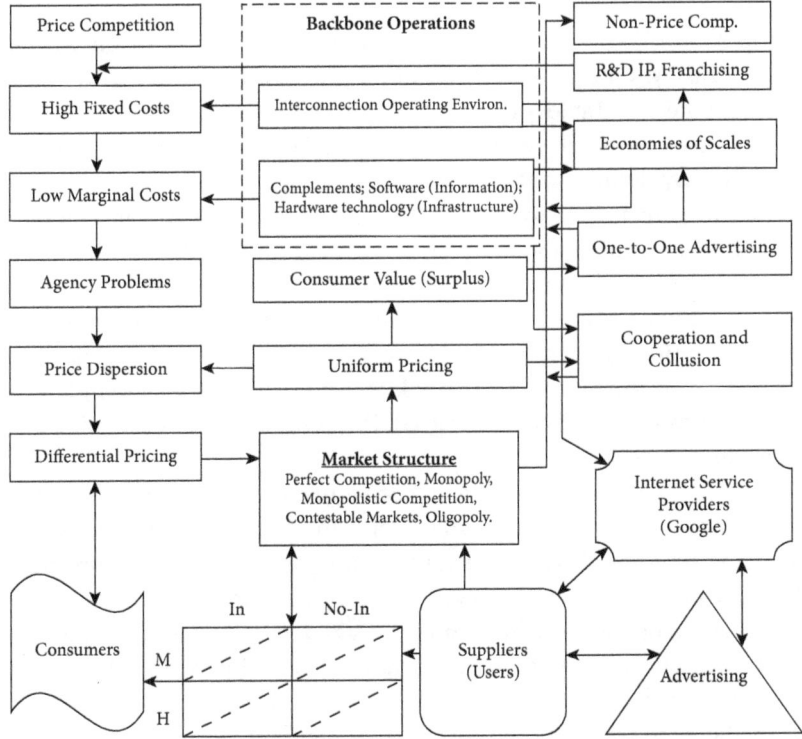

FIGURE 2.1 *Price and nonprice decisions*

outer columns, such as Internet Backbone Providers (IBP) operations, are sandwiched in between. The top half of the figure relates to general discussion in the literature regarding the influence of costs on pricing. The bottom half of the figure shows specific discussion by estimating prices.

One specific discussion in the southeast section of Figure 2.1 captures a model put forth by Hal Varian on YouTube, relating how the players of ISP or Google would like to make the users (book firms) happy by selling them a quality advertising that sells books. Another specific aspect in the SW section tries to capture the pioneering work of Joseph J. Bailey (1998) in relating users (book sellers) through a market (M) and hierarchical (H) arrangement of firms on the Internet (In) and not-Internet (non-In) grid of markets arrangements.

Top half of Figure 2.1

The top half of Figure 2.1 details price and nonprice competition aspects of the industry. One aspect of the dominance of toll revenue by a few firms, as noted in Table 3.1, is that the set-up cost on the Internet can be prohibitive. Another aspect relates to intellectual propriety rights and copyrights. By definition these aspects introduce incentives to innovate, but they also create deadweight loss to consumers, unless the monopolist can price discriminate (Scotchmer, 2004, p. 36). Price discrimination is not easy because consumers can search the web easily to find the lowest price, and even engage in arbitrage. Shapiro and Varian described how price discrimination can be conducted internationally by localizing the information in the text. If a textbook is published in the United States, it can be localized for India using GDP figures in rupees (Shapiro and Varian, 1999, p. 45).

The middle column in the top half of Figure 2.1 shows how innovation affects prices through interconnection and complementary activities. The firms operate in an environment not only to extract consumer surplus from its monopoly power, but also to innovate. We can investigate this phenomenon with a model suggested by Suzanne Scotchmer, which integrates these two aspects simultaneously by the variables (v, c), where the former refers to consumer surplus with competitive supply, and the latter to the cost of innovation (Scotchmer, 2004, p. 39). We can extend this model to show how consumer surplus can be increased to usurp deadweight losses via lower prices through investment in innovation. The IBP box in the figure shows how innovation, as suggested by Mortimer in relation to Table 2.1 discussed earlier, can feed into lower prices. Interconnection and Complementary boxes would translate into less cost and therefore lower prices of the product. The IPS box is another source of innovation to provide price benefits to the consumers. The book industry firms also make R&D expenditures to reduce cost, lower prices, and increase consumer surplus. Amazon's Kindle and Apple's iPad are good examples in this case.

If the hurdle of a high fixed cost is cleared, then the nature of price competition can be assessed. Digitization lowers the marginal costs of firms, and tends to shift competition toward price collusion and into nonprice areas such as service competition. Price dispersion studies tend to show that prices are lower on the Internet, but if a price way is obtained where prices get closer to zero, then agency problem would evolve.

Southeast section of Figure 2.1

According to some analysts, the best way to characterize the pricing of backbone and ISP services is through a "smart market" strategy. The idea is to charge a high price during periods of congestion and a zero usage price during uncongested periods (Mackie-Mason and Varian, 1994, p. 89; Cave and Mason, 2001, p. 196). The underlying idea is that the user will attach a bid for a packet of information he wants to send. For example, an average e-mail contains about 20 packets of information. At congestion time, the packets will be ranked according to bids, and the actual price the user pays is not the offer price, but the lower bid price of the packets that are put through the Internet. MR = MC if all revenue are invested for capacity creation.

Such a smart market bidding process might follow the Vickrey auction process, named in honor of Economics Nobel laureate William Vickrey. In such an auction situation, the sponsor would choose the firm that reports the highest surplus. The winning firm would deliver the innovation to the sponsor for a specified price. In this milieu, firms such as Amazon and Barnes & Noble are likely to have some market power.

As an illustration of Vickrey's auction, consider three bidders, each submitting a bid, say for $10, $8, and $7, respectively. The one that makes the highest bid of $10 will win, but will pay the second highest bid price, $8. Stated differently, say I make a bid, $B = \$10$, but my value of the object for sale is V. Let, $M = \max(\$8, \$7)$ that is, the maximum of the other bids. If $M > V$, then I should set my bid at $B \leq V$; that is, I should not bid more than the value. If $M < V$, then I should set my bid at $B = V$; that is, I should drop the inequality from the previous case because if I bid less then I may not get the object. Bids are submitted simultaneously, and since a bidder cannot affect the price he will pay, there is no incentive to not report the true value. As a theorem, truthful reporting of value is a dominant strategy because whatever the other bidders bid, a particular bidder cannot do better than bidding his true value of the product (Laffront and Tirole, 2002, p. 262). To prove the theorem, assume by contradiction that a player does not bid his value. If he bids less than his value, then he risks losing the item. If he bids more than his value, he can end up with negative profit. Therefore, he would bid his value of the item (He, 2004, p. 13). To avoid regrets in the outcome, one may follow another theorem to the effect that one should bid as though one has won the auction.

Toll price enters as cost to booksellers in setting their price to their customers. As an illustration, consider ad cost pricing through Google to the users. Suppose four bidders offer [$4, $3, $2, $1] respectively for slots [1, 2, 3, 4] with advertising Quality ranking [1, 3, 6, 8]. Cross-multiplying the bids and ad quality yields ad position [4, 9, 12, 8]. We can then use this ad position to rank the bidders as follows: third bidder is first with score 12, second bidder is second place with score 9 and so on. The price that bidder 1 pays, P_1, times the rank position, Q_1, must beat the price bidder two pays, P_2, for its quality rank Q_2. We can now solve the equation $P_1 Q_1 = P_2 Q_2$ for the toll price the first bidder has to pay. This toll price enters as selling cost to the bookseller, and therefore affects the price they set for a book.

The bookseller on the Internet must pay an additional cost, which should be reflected in the marked-up price they set for the consumers. The traditional argument is that higher prices are due to search costs and lack of information about prices. These costs are supposed to be somewhat reduced by the Internet. A pioneering work in this area is Joseph P. Bailey's dissertation. Bailey studied 52 retailers who sold homogenous books and other products through a website on the Internet weekly from February/March 1997 to January 1998. A total of 125 book titles were examined (Bailey, 1998, pp. 79, 82). He found that the mean price on the

Internet was 6.27 percent higher than prices from the physical retailer (ibid., p. 84). There appears to be an anomaly in his study, however, for he counted that prices were lower on the Internet 640 times, greater in the physical retailers 477 times, and the same 601 times for February/March 1997 (ibid., p. 84).

Another aspect of Bailey's study is the dispersion of price. According to the Nobel laureate economist George Stigler, price dispersion is a reflection of "ignorance in the market" (Stigler, 1961, p. 214). The dispersion can be a result of some book dealers rendering more services, carrying a larger stock of books, or selling a heterogeneous or different version of the product. A virtue of the Internet is that it allows the customer to benefit easily from searches for the minimum book price. Stated statistically, the Stigler model advocates that the customer must select as large a sample size of the number of searches until the expected price of the nth search less the expected price of the n+1 search that is equal to the (marginal) cost of an additional search.

Some studies have found no significant difference between the online and conventional prices of books. Studies by Brynjolfsson and Smith (2000), Clay, Krishnan, and Wolff (2001), and Wan (2006) found that price dispersion of online bookstores is not significantly lower than that of conventional bookstores. In summarizing the study of price dispersion, Latcovich and Smith stated this idea more boldly: there is no price competition on the Internet (Latcovich and Smith, 2001, p. 219).

If firms do not compete in pricing, then we must look at nonprice aspects of competition. Firms tend to differentiate their product by providing services and discounts. A look at the 1998 Annual Report for Barnes & Noble.com suggests the following as their nonprice competition offerings: a new software superstore with more than 2,000 titles; one-click ordering; a more powerful search engine that helps customers find any book in print by title, author, keyword, format, subject, price, or ISBN; free e-mail alerts to customers keeping them up to date on their favorite books, subjects, and authors; an expanded selection of bargain books, over 15,000 titles, more than any other online bookseller, discounted up to 90 percent; a cleaner design and shortened download time, enabling shoppers to get where they want faster; an unsurpassed inventory of over six million out-of-print and rare books; access to more than five million newspaper and magazine articles through an agreement with Northern Light Technology; a holiday gift center and a new "Kids!" superstore featuring "Book Boutiques" of children's favorite characters; reader reviews and personal recommendations based on the books customers have purchased; and a handy bookstore locator to find the nearest Barnes & Noble retail store, complete with directions, phone number, and a map.

The issue of price and nonprice aspects is still evolving. It is an attempt to see pricing through traditional market structures encountered in industrial organization and microeconomics. Examples of such historic pricing were done for the mail, telephone, and telegraph systems. It is natural to try and predict Internet pricing from older theories. As the literature suggests, one is not able to predict price behavior through the analysis of market structure as was the case in the old literature. Glimpses of a final pricing theory will come from empirical analysis and case studies, using dynamic programming analysis and game theory where possible.

One simplifying way to recognize pricing is to think of firms setting a flat rate for the customer. Customers will then engage in a search procedure to find the best price. Another way is the time-honored market way, of which an auction system is the closest approximation. The modern literature suggests that auctions play a big role in pricing on the Internet. In this overview, we have shown that ISP provides services to book firms based on the quality of advertising they sell. One implication of ISP pricing to clients is that firms are operating below their minimum efficient size. The cost of the service is determined by an auction. Internet providers use auction price to help booksellers reach their customers. Essentially, a modified version of a Vickrey auction is practiced on the Internet. Firms such as eBay sell all their products through an auction. eBay uses auctions that charge an increment on the next highest bid (Daripa and Kapur, 2001, p. 213). An auction price is attached to each packet, and it takes about 20 packets to send the average e-mail. Auctions, therefore, are costly. The transaction requires resource and time allocation costs, the latter through waiting for a packet to be delivered.

Economies of scale

Once a firm is set up online, it should be able to reach a worldwide market on the network. Economies for the industry would be established if the average cost curve (AC) is falling, which implies that the

TABLE 2.1 *Internet revenue and cost data*

Year	Internet revenue	Average price	Total OP cost	Personnel costs	Material costs	Service costs	Other costs
1998	1.42	5.53					
1999	1.623	5.66					
2000	1.5	6.05					
2001	1.499	6.41					
2002	1.404	6.53					
2003	1.454	6.92					
2004	0.659	5.65	7.011	3.32	0.211	1.298	7.01
2005	0.666	5.48	8.197	3.899	0.249	1.603	8.197
2006	0.714	5.40	8.342	3.78	0.247	1.678	8.341
		5.44					

Sources: Internet revenues are from the Statistical Abstract of the United States—various issues. Average prices are assumed homogenous with conventional price, estimated by census sales/*Statistical Abstract* quantity. Prices are above those of Bowker Mass Media prices, but less than hard- and soft-back prices. Costs are for Publishing and Broadcasting on the Internet.

marginal cost (MC) must be falling at a faster rate. The ratio of AC to MC, therefore, would indicate scale economies if it is greater than unity. This section looks at the online economies for various areas. Table 2.1 indicates Internet book sales and Internet publishing and broadcasting cost data since 2004.

From 2004 to 2006, personnel costs made up approximately 47 percent of total costs, with other services accounting for the next largest share, 31 percent of costs. Purchase services accounted for 19 percent, and material costs were the least, 3 percent of total costs.

Using the fact that MC must fall faster than AC to bring down the long-run average total cost, we estimated that the AC/MC ratio was approximately 4 and 29 in 2005 and 2006, respectively, for operating cost, indicating substantial economies of scale from online activities. During the 2004–2005 period, economies of scale remained very stable for all cost categories—personnel, material, purchased services, and other expenses such as taxes and depreciation, varying from 3 to 5 percent. For the 2005–2006 period, much volatility in the estimates occurred, indicating that economy was to be had from only the latter two categories.

Cost data

Barnes & Noble spent $15.4 million in start-up costs to launch Barnes & Noble.com in 1997 (Annual Report, 1997, p. 6). In 1998, sales increased by

381 percent, from $14.8 to $70.2 million. The company's number of online customers increased by 300 percent, from 313,000 in 1997 to 1,250,000 in 1998, and in-stock inventory increased from 300,000 to 750,000 titles during that period (Annual Report, 1998). This data suggests that increasing return was present at the company level.

Internet bookselling seems to be a contestable market, and ease of entry should be easy. However, we find that only large sellers dominate the market. One can argue that this new branch of the industry seems to fit into Joe Bain's category of price and nonprice competitive oligopoly. The interesting question is whether the firms collude in price and compete in nonprice aspects such as discounts and services.

Middle of Figure 2.1

Toward the middle of Figure 2.1, we list market structure. Shapiro and Varian see the players in the publishing industry as carrying information goods with a differentiated product. The firms' competitive strategy is to add value to their raw information (Shapiro and Varian, 1999, p. 25). The works of Harold Hotelling (1929), Joan Robinson (1933), and Edward Chamberlin (1962) categorize this market structure as monopolistic competition. We can understand this market structure by envisioning a firm selecting a product, say a textbook, and determining its marketing strategy, which in turn leads to profits that attract other firms (Ireland, PD book, 1988, p. 5).

The Nobel laureate economist, Joseph Stiglitz, explained how monopolistic competition works for the sales of textbooks online. Textbooks are differentiated by their size, level, and organization. We can envision more differentiation in the form of macro or micro, for example, a one-semester versus multiple-semester text. Hotelling's model predicts that too many products may concentrate on the center of the market, and too few at the fringes. High-quality books may actually serve as an entry barrier. Successful books are imitated. Clones, versioning, and simplifying books will be developed. New changes have been introduced to make the textbook international and to accommodate changes in the economy (Stiglitz, 1988).

Broadly speaking, book competition takes the form of a game. The players include the End Users, who are residential consumers or businesses; Websites by book publishers or book sellers; and Intermediaries. One type of intermediary provides advice on what products to buy and where to buy them. The Internet provides transmission services through ISP (Internet service providers, such as AOL) or IBP (such as CI-World. com) (Laffront and Tirole, 2002, p. 269).

Southeast of Figure 2.1

The south section of Figure 2.1 highlights consumer behavior and activities on the Internet. Data from ComScore on media metrics allows analysis of consumers' search patterns on the Internet. One can test hypotheses regarding sequential versus nonsequential searches, on the assumption of known and unknown price distribution of books on the Internet. Price information from such data sources represents another source of elasticity and mark-up measures for the book industry online.

Babur De los Santos, Ali Hortacsu, and Matthijs R. Wildenbeest have done such a study with ComScore and mySimon.com data (Santos et al., 2009). They reported results for 15 online bookstores, including Amazon.com (66 percent of transactions), Barnes & Noble (20 percent), and book clubs (11 percent) for 7,558 observations during June–December of 2002, and 8,020 observations in 2004. "Approximately 38 percent of the users realized a product transaction in 2002 (48 percent of users in 2004), and 7 percent of users bought at least one book online in 2002 (10 percent in 2004)" (ibid., 5).

To conclude this overview, we see the book industry competing in two layers: bookstores and the Internet. We see the traditional weapons of competition, such as advertising and the number of stores, as strategies that are still significant. We see that nonprice competition has been particularly elevated. Digital technology has revolutionized the ways of the industry with regard to both supply and demand.

Demand and supply: theoretical aspects

The market for books is undergoing a revolution. Although the new market paradigm does not quite usurp the traditional brick-and-mortar approach, traditional bookstores are in a survival-of-the-fittest mode of competition within the Internet domain. The market for e-books is not in a win-win relation with the market for print books. If anything, they are in a zero-sum game relation where the increased share of e-books is gained at the expense of the print books market share. New trends include the following:

- Libraries where the information and knowledge of civilization are stored for current and future generations now provide web access to their patrons.
- Colleges that were looking for alternative ways to lower the costs of college texts have changed their syllabi to allow e-books for students.
- The digital technology that allows print-on-demand has lightened the cost of inventory of books.
- Easy access to books via the Internet has intensified competition between the markets for used and new books.
- The evolution of e-books has created a new medium in which to read. In 2007, Amazon rolled out the Kindle e-reader, and Apple followed with the iPad, iTouch, iPhone, and iBookstore. In December 2010, Barnes & Noble debuted their own e-reader, the Nook.
- Easier access and simplified procedures for self-publishing have eliminated the middleman. In cyberspace, you can publish your manuscript within several days.
- There's rivalry resembling zero-sum game, in which e-book sales are accompanied by a decline in print book sales. The continuous drop in print book sales was the major cause of the failure of Borders Bookstore. (Bowker Annual Report, 2011, p. 451)

Basically, the new market paradigm of the book industry represents a supply or technological shock on the supply side. On the demand side, consumers can now search for bargains, and can choose among different ways to allocate their time when reading a book. Readers now have to choose between allocating time to new reading gadgets versus game-play gadgets. Traditional microeconomic theory predicts higher utility for their better choices. The increasing popularity of e-readers, in accordance with the time-honored law of demand, has increased e-book purchases, and allowed substitution of e-books for print books.

Demand for books results in human capital accumulation

The predominant view is that the demand for a book is like the demand for any commodity for which the law of demand applies. Alongside that view is a predominant inclination to take into account the new ideas developed in the latter half of the 20th century, that a book contributes to human capital accumulation. The demand for a book is in large part a demand to build human capital. A human capital approach requires us to treat the demand for books as a demand for a factor of production. Alfred Marshall, a major classical economist, was not indifferent to this analysis when he wrote that "human faculties are as important a means of production as any other kind of capital" (Marshall, 1982, p. 191).

Models of human capital compare income streams generated from entering the workforce with human capital possessing different levels of education and experience. More education is generally associated with more benefits, but there is an optimal level of human capital, say about two years beyond high school. As books contribute to the embodied knowledge of a worker, such human capital is linked with technological efficiency. This efficiency is captured in production functions, such as in the Solow Residual of the neoclassical production function, amounting to an upward drift in the production function.

Books enter as a direct expense in human capital accumulation. A simple measure of human capital is one's age less schooling, less experience, or on-the-job training. For example, if a person is 22 years old, entered kindergarten at age 5, and just completed high school, then a measure of his human capital is: HC = 22 − 12 − 5 = 5. Human capital varies with time and can be written as $h(t)$ following Lucas (Lucas, 2002, p. 35).

A first refinement of $h(t)$ is to show that it does not accrue for all types of reading of a book. One author classified education into four purposes: not very near future productivity, very near future productivity, pleasure in the near future, and pleasure at present. Human capital "is created through educational investment...To the extent that education is to produce current (present) pleasures...it will be characterized as consumption" (Machlup, 1962, p. 115).

In general, the modern literature carries the definition of the human capital problem as the production of two commodities. One commodity, c_{1t}, will be produced for the market, while another commodity, c_{2t}, is produced for entertainment or leisure (Sargent, 1987, pp. 52–53). A person's demand, therefore, comes out of a utility function with these two inputs: $U(c_{1t}, c_{2t})$. The explicit form of this function varies. Robert Lucas, Jr., recommended a CES type of utility function (Lucas, 2002, p. 48). Gylfason recommends the Cobb-Douglas function for endogenous growth problems (Gylfason, 2003, p. 138). Samuelson has recommended the HARA of CRRA type, which we will discuss in the following pages. A person's demand for books must first solve the allocation problem between the consumption and human capital aspects of demand.

Demand of books for the production of human capital for the market will depend on the market wage rate, w_t. The wage rate will determine how much time the buyer of a book will allocate its reading for the purpose of producing human capital for the market, l_{1t}. The budget constraint for this aspect of reading will therefore be $c_{1t} \leq w_t l_{1t}$.

Demand of books for entertainment or leisure will depend on the expertise of a book's buyer at the outset, say a_t. The budget constraint for this activity will be $c_{2t} \leq f(a_t)$. Stock usually depreciates, say by a rate of δ, and can be increased by allocating more labor to its production.

To put this model of human capital to work, we need to specify its laws of motion with regard to the wage rate on the demand side, and with regard to the accumulation of expertise on the supply side. The wage rate will evolve in a recursive manner; $w_{t+1} = h(w_t)$. The stock of expertise will also evolve recursively $a_{t+1} = (1 - \delta) a_t + l_{2t}$.

The overall model we describe is a regular consumer maximization problem, faithful to the formulation of Thomas Sargent, where the consumer is maximizing a utility function subject to two budget constraints, the laws of motion, a positive stock of expertise, and the conversation of labor input. A solution can be attempted through the Lagrange multiplier process, or the problem can be tackled in subparts using dynamic programming analysis.

We observe that the two components of demand in the book industry are not always recognized in the literature. It is slightly different from the overall view of education where "Most of the outlays for education can be regarded as investment in human capital because they are expected to yield returns in future years" (Machlup, 1962, p. 63). Books are broadly classified into categories such as trade, professional, and college. Even the mighty IRS, recognizing that a book's cost is an investment, allows some deductions for book expenses for college students and professionals. But the IRS will not allow a deduction for a book that does not serve as an investment in human capital. That is not to say that pleasure reading is unimportant. To the extent that pleasure reading enhances social welfare, it may have positive externalities.

We also observe that the literature speaks of two types of human capital: general and specific, and "persons receiving general training would be willing to pay these costs since training raises their future wages"

(Becker, 1993, p. 34). This happens when you buy a book. "Resources are usually spent by firms...and the knowledge thus acquired is a form of specific training because productivity is raised more in the firms acquiring the knowledge than in other firms" (ibid., p. 41). This occurs when the employer or someone else buys books for you, being interested in your skills.

Components of demand

If one were to draw the demand curve for the book industry, then the components of demand of the two commodities, c_{1t} and c_{2t} should be spelled out in their different time aspects for further analysis. We can now write out the varying time aspect of the components of demand in equation form:

$$D_k = B_{c,pr} + B_{c,nfr} + B_{i,,fr,} + B_{i,nfr} \qquad (Eq\ 2.1)$$

Where pr is present time, fr is future time, nfr is near future time, c is consumption, i is investment, B is book, k is stock, and D is demand. Here, r is used as the time variable to be consistent with Keynes's discount model, which is discussed in the following paragraphs.

Since a person's taste and preference are given, then present consumption, the first term in equation 2.1, is an exogenous variable. The rest of the demand determinants are all for the future and therefore have a discount component. Following Keynes, the gain to the human capital builder is the prospective yield, Q_r, where r is time. To estimate the present value of the buyer, we apply the discount rate, d_r. The aggregate demand price will be $\Sigma Q_r d_r$ (Keynes, 1936, p. 137). The discount rate may be given here. One can imagine a situation where reading or purchasing a book for human capital purposes will continue until the present value from the purchase exceeds the present value from forgoing the investment: PV(book consumption) > PV(without book consumption)

Such a demand curve is shown in Figure 2.2. The figure is adapted from Paul Davidson's market model for capital accumulation, and therefore subject to similar shift parameters (Davidson, 1969, p. 308). The parameter of such a demand curve will depend on the price of books, the interest rate for discounting the human capital components of demand, and buyer expectation about the future prospects of reading.

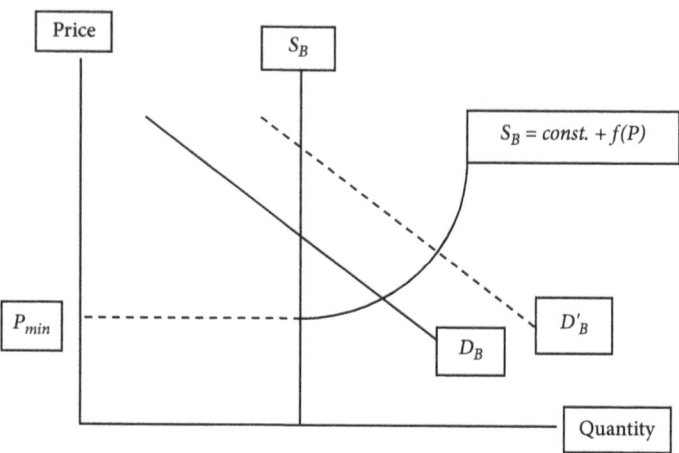

FIGURE 2.2   *Supply and demand for books*

The supply of books is given simply as an accumulated stock, fixed for a time period.

The comparative static aspects of the market should be considered as well. Supply will consider a minimum shut down price, P_{min}, in Figure 2.2. For instance, the main problem of Borders Bookstore was the falling demand for print books in competition with e-books, depressing prices so much that the company (with its brick-and-mortar stores and lack of a full-service website) was put out of business. One can therefore represent the flow of supply curve as $SB = constant + f(Price)$.

Behavior of demand over time

The consideration of human capital formation in the book market increases the complexity of demand and supply analysis over time. Paul Samuelson has given us two hypotheses to consider in this regard.

> **Hypothesis 1:** *The capitalized (present discounted) value of the human capital declines as I (readers) age and as my (their) age in retirement shrinks.* (Samuelson, 2011, 7:101)

The discounted aspect clearly excludes the first component of demand in eq(1). One does not discount pleasure in present time, and people read for pleasure at all ages. It has only limited applicability for the other three time-designated components of the equation as well. Someone who retires early goes on to another job where he continues reading. Those who retire on time may find it convenient to continue to read to keep abreast with new developments, and today's Internet technology facilitates this endeavor with ease.

This hypothesis has an age component. One can appreciate that at different ages, particularly during the student years, the cost of books can be a significant expenditure comprising a large percentage of one's current income. Students often go into debt, borrowing from future income to accommodate this expense. Firms pick up this expense when they provide training, perhaps to lighten their costs of employee turnover, for efficiency wage causes, or just to enhance productivity.

Hypothesis 2: *The presence of nonrisky human capital also raises people's equity tolerance.* (Ibid., p. 103)

This hypothesis incorporates the financial aspects of human capital. The gain is to maximize some utility when facing the direct cost of book expenditures. This analysis has risk bearing in a life cycle setting where one is uncertain as to the payoff of the investment. Samuelson suggested that "in your prime of life you have the same relative risk-tolerance as toward the end of life" (Samuelson, 1972, 3:889). Risk tolerance is measured by the second derivative of a utility function of wealth or consumption. We have already noted that a part of consumption of books in present time is excluded in this analysis. The analysis, therefore, is applicable to the future accumulation of knowledge through book consumption. For those future book purchases, if the second derivative of risk tolerance is positive, the investor is risk averse, and if it is negative, then the investor is a risk lover. If the second derivative is scaled by the first derivative, then we get an absolute value of risk. Taking the inverse of that gives a measure of risk tolerance. Multiplying the absolute value of risk by the consumption or wealth gives a relative value of risk (Arrow, 1984, 3:151).

What utility function does a buyer want to maximize? Samuelson constructed his theory of long-term investment in a utility mold. Risk tolerance is of the linear form $-\dfrac{U'(C)}{U''(C)} = a + bC$, which includes exponential, logarithmic, quadratic, and hyperbolic special cases. The exponential special case over time $U(C,t) = e^{-\rho t} V(C)$ turns into a Hyperbolic Absolute Risk Aversion (HARA) by making $V(C) = \dfrac{1-\gamma}{\gamma}\left(\dfrac{aC}{1-\gamma} + b\right)^{\gamma}$, which includes unbounded utility functions (Morton, 1970, p. 18). The exponential special case $U(C, t) = C^r$ is a Constant Relative Risk Aversion (CRRA), which deals with investments irrespective of a person's age. For the restrictions $r < 0$; $r = 0$, and $r > 0$, the relative risk function is $\frac{1-r}{C}$, and the same result is obtained if one adds constants and slopes to the exponential special case (Walker, 2008, p. 1339).

To summarize this section, the consumer wants to maximize a utility function, $U(C_{1t}, C_{2t})$, which can be specified as a CES, Cobb-Douglas, HARA, or CRRA type. The constraints facing the individual are budget constraints, law of motions for wages and stock of expertise, labor, and nonnegative constraints. The problem is typically solved by Lagrangian multipliers, or subdivided for Dynamic Programming analysis. The equilibrium prices are obtained from a search procedure, which we now describe.

Demand and search costs

The direct cost of books from the human capital angle can be affected by the search cost the buyer has incurred. Assume the consumer is looking for a book. Different sellers on the web will list the book for different prices. One can make up a table of price distribution showing the number of dealers within each price range (Stigler, 1961, p. 214). Shop bots like mySimon.com and websites like Addall.com allow you to find and compare a number of dealers selling a given book.

Prices may vary across different websites for many reasons. A seller may provide different services, carry a large stock, or may be passing on discounts from the publisher. One can, therefore, classify sites by their different price ranges. Stigler's static example considers sellers as grouped within only two price ranges that include minimum prices of $2 and $3. If a buyer makes only one search, he will face a 50:50 chance (0.5 probabilities each) of reaching each minimum, yielding an expected payoff of $E(B) = .5(2) + .5(3) = \$2.5$. Since the highest price is $3, the buyer's expected savings will be 50 cents (Stigler, 1961, p. 214). As the buyer makes more searches, the probability will vary, making it more probable to get a lower price, and increasing the expected savings with each search.

A simple statistical model can start from the assumption that prices are uniformly distributed within a price range. Statistical theory states that as one makes many sampling from a uniform distribution, the result converges to a normal distribution. To explain the sampling procedure to find a minimum price, let p be the probability of drawing $2 from one price range, then $(1 - p)$ will be the probability of getting the $3 price. As the search proceeds for n periods, the Maximum Likelihood Estimate is $L(p;n) = p^1(1 - p)^{n-1}$. In that illustration, $n = 2$ For larger values of n and sampling from a normal distribution, the MLE estimate of the average minimum price is derived through the following steps. First one starts with the probability density functions (PDF) for the normal distribution.

$$f(p) = \frac{1}{\sqrt{2\pi\delta^2}} e^{-\frac{1}{2}\left(\frac{(p-\mu)^2}{\delta^2}\right)}$$

If we are interested in finding the MLE of the variance, given the mean, then we can rewrite it as follows:

$$f(p;\delta^2) = \frac{1}{\sqrt{2\pi\delta^2}} \exp\left[-\frac{(p-\mu)^2}{2\delta^2}\right]$$

Taking n samples with known means and unknown variances for several samples ($n > 1$) would multiply these density functions, because the samplings are independent from each other. So, the MLE functions for the samples appear as products.

$$f(p_1,\cdots,p_n;\delta^2) = \frac{1}{\sqrt{2\pi\delta^2}} \exp\left[-\frac{(p-\mu)^2}{2\delta^2}\right] \times \frac{1}{\sqrt{2\pi\delta^2}} \exp\left[-\frac{(p-\mu)^2}{2\delta^2}\right]\cdots$$

Or more compactly, one can write:

$$= f(p_1,\cdots,p_n;\delta^2) = \left(\frac{1}{\sqrt{2\pi\delta^2}}\right)^n \prod_{n=1}^{n} \exp\left[-\frac{(p-\mu)^2}{2\delta^2}\right]$$

Sampling in this way, one can cumulate the probability of finding the average price by taking the integral, yielding a cumulative density function (CDF):

$$\int_a^b f(p) = F_p.$$

In the search process, one finds the minimum price by the usual procedure of setting the first derivative equal to zero and solving for the minimum price. One incurs a cost, c, in the process. Such a cost may have a distribution, F_c. In some recent empirical work, the procedure employed was to find a price of a book that would minimize the search cost. One such function for nonsequential search procedure is as follows:

$$\ell^*(c) = Arg\min_{\ell>1} c(\ell-1) + \int_{\underline{p}}^{\bar{p}} \ell p \left(1 - F_p(p)\right)^{\ell-1} f(p) dp$$

In that equation, one first obtains a random sample of prices, $l > 1$ The incurred cost is c. Prices and costs are drawn from statistical distributions, F_p and F_c, respectively. This is, therefore, a two-parameter search problem: $(l;c)$. Argmin tells the computer what to return from the expression, namely, the price that would minimize the cost of the search. Hong and Shum's 2006 study focused on how to estimate F_c using only a sample of random prices drawn from F_p.

Hong and Shum have also given examples of sequential search procedures. In their case the consumer has a reservation price with which it compares a price discovered from every step in the search. They allow the recovery of the cost from the price distribution and have made additional assumptions in defining the PDF and associated CDF for the sequential search procedure (Hong and Shum, 2006, pp. 264–265). The additional assumptions led them to consider the more flexible GAMMA distribution for estimation purposes. In their conclusion, the authors recognize the limitations of their model, including sellers' bait-and-switch strategies, adverse selection problems as buyers are not able to inspect the product before purchase, and delays in delivery.

Some purchases, such as those made on eBay, are priced through auction. Adam Smith said that in an auction situation, "if two persons have an equal fondness for a book, He whose fortune is largest will carry it" (Smith 1978, 5:496). As profound as the statement appears, the modern market for books may have changed since Smith made his observation. These days, anyone can buy books that are being sold on the auction-based Internet. As we shall see in the Internet chapter, publishers themselves buy space on the Internet through an auction procedure. One of the biggest features the Internet has to offer is competitive discounting, of both agency and retailer types.

The ability to digitize books now provides a plethora of supply options. This new element has given rise to some dominant firms such as Amazon, Barnes & Noble, and Books-a-Million on the web. The success of a dominant firm is based on efforts to block entry of its rivals, which can take many avenues. We observed that dominant firms in the e-book markets have some market power on price fixing. For instance, Amazon entered the e-reader/e-book market in 2009 with a low price of $9.99. We can look at that pricing as a two-tiered structure reflecting a wholesale pricing model between publisher and seller, where the seller sells for double the price that the publisher wants. One observes also an agent model, where the principal (the publisher) sets the price, and the agent (the seller) gets a fixed commission.

Figure 2.3, adopted from Viscusi et al. (2005, p. 65), shows the resulting price discrimination occurring among the dominant firms around 2011. Publishers observe that Amazon's pricing for e-books is somewhat low, perhaps because Amazon wants to block entry into that space. One can see an analogy here for the antitrust case of Microsoft trying to

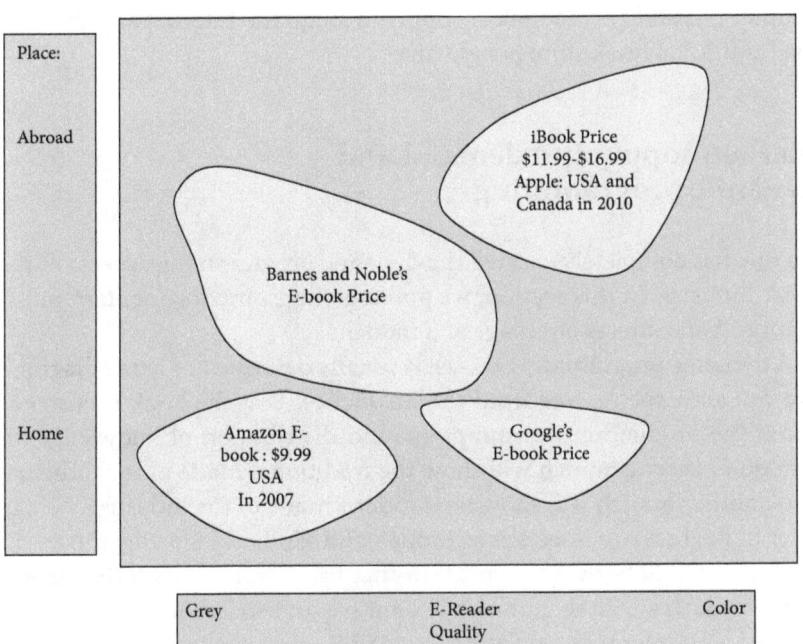

FIGURE 2.3 *Product versus spatial differentiation of the e-book market*

block entry in the browsers' market by lowering the price of its Internet Explorer to zero.

At first the joint supply of e-books and e-readers created a complementary relation in supply. E-books could originally be downloaded only on e-readers. But later, the advent of Google e-books, made available through Google's cloud digital technology, shattered that complement model, allowing e-books to be read from almost all reading devices. This suggests that the competitors had no choice but to make better-quality e-readers and sell them at a higher price, as portrayed in Figure 2.3 (Bowker, 2011, pp. 3, 11).

The Internet now pits the seller in more intensive competition, which results in more discounts. One is tempted to say that instead of the "poor man's son" parable of deception, we have a "seller deception" (Smith 1978, 5:181), as sellers move to the Internet and continue to impact their brick-and-mortar rivals. The new breed of competitors such as Amazon, which have both feet in the Internet market and no interest in physical stores, are faring better and gaining shares in the industry.

One can start the supply of books analysis by looking at two segments. One segment has a stock component, while the other does not. Yet another possibility is to look at supply through the Internet and through the traditional book store perspective.

Market: supply and demand and dynamic programming

No one has completely charted the dynamic programming aspects of the book industry. In this section, we pull together some fragmentary information that conjures an image of a model.

A dynamic programming model is usually described by a tree diagram. We can start such a tree from the distinction that the book industry is about the production, consumption, and distribution of knowledge. In that domain, one branch will show the traditional mode of the industry, and another branch will show the modern mode of the industry. We can refer to the first two branches as Mode 1 and Mode 2, following the works of Gibbons (Gibbons, 2004, p. 1). In that framework, the Mode 1 aspect of the industry will be guided by cognitive and social norms, while the Mode 2 aspect is more "socially accountable and reflexive." While Mode 1 leans toward the academic, Mode 2 leans toward applicability. Mode 1 is

Overview of Price and Nonprice Competition   39

disciplinary and Mode 2 is transdisciplinary. Mode 1 is homogenous and Mod 2 is heterogeneous. Mode 1 is hierarchical and Mode 2 is heterarchical (ibid., p. 3). These terms are useful for the whole knowledge industry, but must be made more specific for the book industry.

Looking at the Mode 1 characteristics of the book industry, one finds an emphasis on bookstores' activities. Firms may display behavioral tendencies that underscore willingness or hesitancy to move toward the Internet. Following the classification schema of Figure 2.4 to study firms' behavior, it is clear that Amazon will be placed in Mode 2. The traditional bookstore firms such as Barnes & Noble and Books-a-Million will be placed in Mode 1, with a limb extended to the Internet.

In the northeast corner of Figure 2.4, we can consider cases where traditional brick-and-mortar bookstores may want to become reflexive. The term *reflexivity* was used by George Soros in his 1987 book *The Alchemy of Finance*, suggesting in a methodological sense that the world is fallible, and that the actions that arise from such a world are reflexive. Competition in the book industry is reflexive in this sense. Traditional book companies started a trend with "super bookstores," and the rest followed. As we have shown earlier, that activity did not pay off for Borders, as its sales were negatively correlated with superstore expansion.

Figure 2.4 also forces us to think of the struggle of Germany and the Internet. One view is that Germany wanted to preserve its legacy in printing and was therefore hesitant to embrace the Internet. Traditional

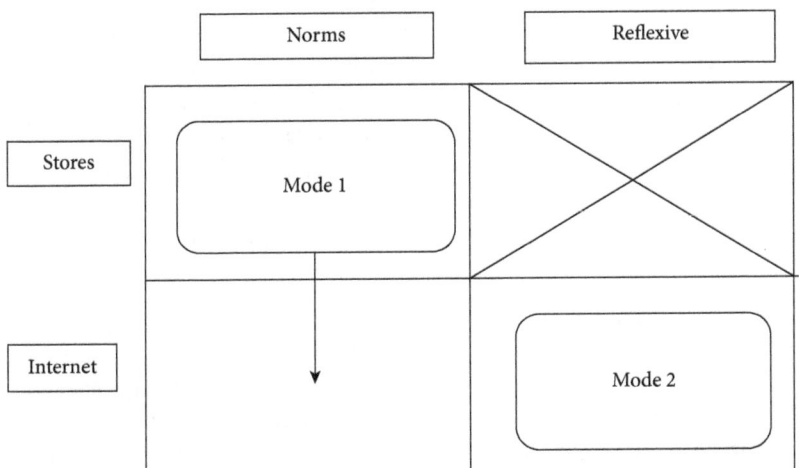

FIGURE 2.4   *Dynamic view of the book industry*

price theory predicts that a player (firm or country) would benefit from the movement toward the Internet. In fact, it is now textbook knowledge that Amazon and B&N are brand names for fast and reliable service, and that new sellers will have to embrace the Internet to compete.

An important feature unique to Mode 1 supply is that sellers need to carry a fixed inventory. We start with the assumption that at any given time, a stock of capital exists

$$S_k = a_k \qquad (Eq2.2)$$

where S is supply, a is a stock of books that exist at a point in time. For firms that hold inventory, one can follow Arrow et al. (1958, p. 19) in specifying a model for inventory behavior, which spans problems relating to scheduling, production, distribution, replacement, and pricing. Economic models have evolved more in some areas than in others for dealing with the problem. In a continuous time period setting, one may write out an equation for the changes in the stock as follows:

$$dS_k / dt = z(t) - r(t) \qquad (Eq2.2a)$$

The equation 2.2a explains how equation 2.2 may adjust over time. It says that the rate of change in stock is a difference between orders and the amount sold. From this equation, we can get the stock, S_k, by integration. Amazon "endeavor[s] to accurately predict these trends and avoid overstocking or understocking products...Demand for products, however, can change significantly between the time inventory or components are ordered and the date of sale" (Amazon Annual Report, 2008, p. 12). Barnes & Noble employs an inventory database called BookMaster, which "allows the Company to achieve high in-stock positions and productivity at the store level through efficiencies in receiving, cashiering and returns processing" (Barnes & Noble Annual Report, 2012, p. 10). Books-a-Million ships a substantial part of its inventory to its subsidiary, American Wholesale, which has locations in Tuscumbia and Florence, Alabama.

> Orders from our bookstores are processed by computer and assembled for delivery to the stores on pre-determined weekly schedules. Substantially all deliveries of inventory from American Wholesale's facilities are made by a dedicated transportation fleet. At the time deliveries are made to each of our stores, returns of slow-moving or obsolete products are picked up and returned to the American Wholesale returns processing center. American

Wholesale then returns these products to vendors for credit, if credit is available. (Ibid., p. 10)

Bringing demand and supply together

One way to bring the two sides of the market together is through game theory. This can be done by invoking the cateris paribus assumption of (1) fixing demand and varying supply or (2) fixing supply and varying demand. These aspects can be viewed from the perspective of game theory.

The Nobel laureate Reinhard Selten has developed *The Chain Store Paradox* game that we can use in this regard (Selten, 1978). Barnes & Noble has a chain of stores located in n geographical areas. It faces potential entry from its rivals. The potential entrants will enter sequentially, in the sense that ith entrant will observe what happened in the i-1 preceding markets. Each entrant's pure strategies are either "enter (In)" or "stay out (Out)." If a rival enters, the existing firm (incumbent) decides whether to cooperate or not to cooperate with the entrant.

In order to bring out the salient characteristics of the chain store game, we have graphed Selten's example on a decision tree (Selten, 1978, p. 129). On the upper branch of Figure 2.5, we show that the entrant will guarantee itself a payoff of 1, whether the incumbent plays with a cooperative or aggressive strategy. One could collapse this upper branch to show the same payoff of (5,1) for each of the incumbent strategies, but that is not necessary.

On the lower branch, Figure 2.5, a firm enters a local area, and the incumbent reacts by either cooperating or not cooperating. If the incumbent cooperates, then both players get the same payoff of (2,2) If the entrant does not cooperate, then both players will lose, getting (0,0). Selten makes the seemingly paradoxical observation that "In the short run the COOPERATIVE response is more advantageous but in the long run it may pay to choose the AGGRESSIVE response in order to discourage the choice of IN" (Selten, 1978, p. 130).

Selten calls the short-run view inductive, and the long-run view deterrent, and proceeds to examine repeated plays under a prisoner's dilemma setting. He considers three levels on which this game should be played—using experience from present and past decisions, using imaginations as in simulation, and with consideration of rational strategies.

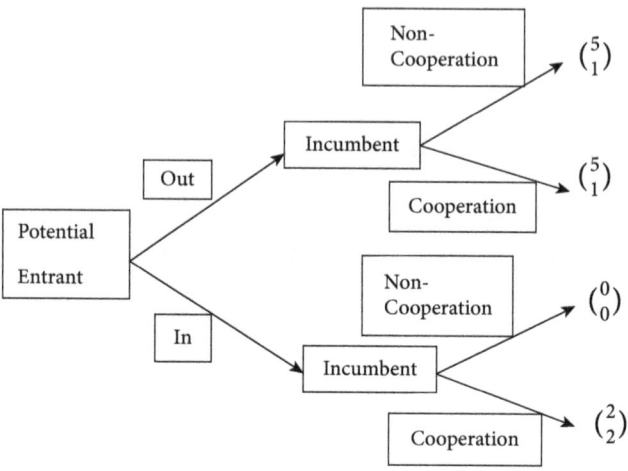

FIGURE 2.5   *The Chain Store Paradox*
Source: Adopted from Selten, 1978, p. 129.

Fixing demand versus varying supply

Competition in chain stores is natural for the expansion of a business. "When a merchant has corralled the bulk of the business of the territory within a trading radius of his store...The natural thing is to open a branch store at some nearby point outside of competition with the first store...in the end there is a chain of stores under one management" (Farrington, 1922, pp. 5–6). Among the advantages of a chain store are the ability to weed out inefficient independent competitors (ibid., p. 10) and allow a firm to support some branch stores temporarily even if they are operating at a loss (ibid., 27).

A survey of chain store performance over the past century was done by Miller, who studied the case of Macy's efforts at price maintenance in the face of price rivalry. The American Booksellers Association (ABA) was founded in 1900 to help defend the idea that prices must be maintained at the low level established by book publishers. It asked booksellers to guarantee a minimum price. But Macy's, whose strategy was to underprice its competitors, did not go along with the ABA's guidelines, and sued the ABA in 1902 for restraining competition. In 1913, the courts ruled in favor of Macy's (Miller, 2006, p. 154).

The issue of price discrimination was a major concern for the chain store game in the 1930s. It was elevated to an amendment of the Clayton

Antitrust Act by the Robinson-Patman Act in 1936. Its relevance to the book industry surfaced in 1994, when the ABA and some independent bookstores complained against several companies, including Houghton Mifflin Company, Penguin USA, and St. Martin's Press. The complaint was made in the New York courts under the Robinson-Patman Act on the grounds that the defendants were giving more promotional allowances and price discounts to larger national chains and clubs. In 1998, the ABA again filed complaints in California against Barnes & Noble and the now extinct Borders Group on a similar matter. Apparently, the introduction of superstores empowered competition from the independents in the 1990s. The independent sellers fought back from their trade organization base, invoking antitrust laws and beefing up educational campaigns to attract customers (Miller, 2006, p. 163).

To further illustrate the chain store game, we can look at the case of Barnes & Noble as the incumbent and Borders as the entrant. Barnes & Noble was aware of the rules regarding "Area of Dominant Influence" (ADI). As of February 1, 1997, Barnes & Noble had 132 stores in 208 ADI markets. At that time, superstores were beginning to grow, but only numbered 61 in those markets. Barnes & Noble began creating their own superstores in 1990 (Barnes & Noble Annual Report, 1997, p. 5).

Apparently, Barnes & Noble's superstores were not profitable at first, for the company reported that "For the first time since the 'super' store rollout began in 1990 we posted operating profits in all of our fiscal quarters. Operating profit of $147.3 million reflected a 23% increase over 1996, and as a percentage of revenues, grew to 5.3% from last year's 4.9%" (Barnes & Noble Annual Report, 1997, p. 4). Profits were enhanced from the launching of BarnesandNoble.com in May 1997, and the expansion of its distribution center that year to service all its distribution channels: retail stores, Internet sales, 1-800-THE BOOK, and mail order.

Meanwhile, in 1999, Borders' strategy was to dismiss the notion that "physical retail stores are dead in a .com world." Borders opened 46 new domestic superstores that year, focusing on a retail convergence strategy defined as "the integration of traditional and emerging retail channels" (Borders Annual Report, 1999, p. 2). Borders operated the Internet group Borders.com and was active in expanding its "Borders Group Fulfillment Center" to serve its Borders stores, Borders.com, and Waldenbooks customers. As shown earlier, its expansion in the superstores area and sales revenues per square foot declined.

Books-a-Million operates on the Internet at www.booksamillion.com, as well as under four distinct store formats: large superstores operating under the names Books-A-Million and Books & Co., as well as traditional bookstores and combination book and greeting card stores (Books-a-Million Annual Report, 1999). The company has specifically targeted the southeastern United States as its area of operation. Books-a-Million operates in only 17 states and has strong distribution subsidiaries, such as American Wholesale Book Company, Inc, American Internet Services, Inc., and NetCentral, Inc.

Judging from the discussions so far, for Barnes & Noble, Borders, and Books-a-Million, chain and superstore competition seems to be returning low profits and can be placed in the noncooperative strategy from the incumbent side. In that strategy, incumbents aim to prevent entrants from driving profits downward through competition. The profits-enhancing strategy in the chain store game has been a focus in strengthening the companies' distribution centers to service their customers. Amazon.com, which does not compete in stores, has especially demonstrated the need for a strong distribution strategy. In 1997, Amazon's distribution center capacity grew from 50,000 to 285,000 square feet when it expanded its Seattle facilities by 70 percent, and opened a second location in Delaware (Amazon Annual Report, 1997).

Varying demand and supply

On the supply side, there are now an unprecedented number of ways to produce a book. With the new ability to print books on demand, suppliers save tremendously on storage space, and e-books do not require shelf space at all.

On the demand side, we can look at niches such as reading for pleasure, $c(t)$, and reading for human capital formation, $h(t)$. Those aspects of demand can be accommodated by reading on devices such as the Kindle, Nook, iPhone, iPad, or computer.

The changing demand and supply relationships seem to be related as a feedback mechanism over time. From reading books, k, the consumer gets a flow of income from its human capital realization, say $y_k = \theta_t k_t$, where θ represents a proportional constant. Such income can allow increased purchases of books either for consumption needs, $c(t)$, and/or human capital formation, $h(t)$. In a dynamic stochastic programming context, the buyer will face different states of the world and would choose an alternative based on personal probability. Over time, a path on a decision tree would emerge as the one that maximizes the consumer's utility, either continuously or discretely over time.

Dynamic programming aspects of demand

One can specify a dynamic programming model for this process in simple form. On the demand side, the consumer maximizes an expected utility function in discrete form:

$$E_0 \sum_{t=0}^{T} u[c(t), h(t)] \beta_t,$$

where E is the expectation operator, u is the two component utility function, β is a discount factor, where the consumer lives in the time interval t to T. The consumer is maximizing that function subject to its income constraint, which varies with regard to its proportional constants, θ over time, and the consumer stock of books, $y_k = \theta_t k_t$. The solution to the consumer maximization problem can therefore be written as $B(t, \theta_t, k_t)$, which accounts for the varying parameters on book demand. In the consumer model, one can apply a rate of depreciation to the stock, k_t.

The performance of the book industry indicates increased production and consumption of books over time. One can surmise that the changing demand and supply parameters are evolving in an outward spiraling fashion. The reach of technology to overseas markets has fed that spiral during the globalization period, without saturating the market.

On the producer's side, we need a production function to reflect the influence of technology. One challenge is how to represent exogenous technology, where the technology of one firm affects the output of another firm.

Dynamic programming aspects of supply

One concern with the dynamic side of supply is embedded in the idea that the supply of books is the supply of knowledge. This raises the question of whether technology is internal or external to book publishing. The return to a new idea of production does not accrue only to the originator of an idea, and is therefore external to the company that originates the idea (Lucas, 2002, p. 4).

Exogenous growth

The traditional neoclassical model deals with exogenous growth. Take a Cobb-Douglas specification for output $Y(t) = A(t)\left[L(t)^{\alpha} K(t)^{(1-\alpha)}\right]$, where Y, t, L, K, a refers to output, time, labor, capital, and returns to scale, respectively. Given the $K(t)$, $A(t)$, $L(t)$ for a given time period, one needs to choose consumption over time to maximize utility (Lucas, 2000, p. 25).

Endogenous growth

Another aspect of the dynamics of supply is that its technology is not exogenous but endogenous. One can think of this as a "learning by doing" process, which would translate to the idea that output is proportional to capital, since labor learns from the use of capital. Therefore, if we write, $Y = aK$ where Y is book output, K is capital in the book industry, and a is the marginal product of capital.

Endogenous growth theorists postulate the marginal product of K (MPK) is constant, not diminishing returns as postulated in standard neoclassical theories. Constant MPK means that if a firm doubles capital then its output will also double. The result is that as capital is augmented with other factors such as labor and materials, increasing returns to scales will result. For instance, the marginal product of labor (MPL) would be positive, so $MPK + MPL > 1$ which indicates increasing returns (Dornbusch et al., 2004, p. 81; Gylfason, 2003, p. 138).

If the firms are supplying books under conditions of increasing returns, then the larger the firm, the more efficient it will be—which predicts that a monopoly will result. The appearance of giants such as Amazon and Barnes & Noble may seem a corroboration of this hypothesis. But others have suggested that other factors are at play.

The work of Paul Romer underscores a distinction between private and social returns. He conceives a production function of the form $F(A, X)$ where A is the firm's own inputs and X is other firms' inputs. This way the industry's capital enters a firm's production function. In such a function, if a firm were to increase its ideas' capital by a certain percent, its output would increase by more than that percent. The increasing returns depend on the influence of the social capital, because the individual producer faces diminishing returns to its own capital (Romer, 1990, p. S76; Lucas, 2002, p. 4). This avoids the tendency toward monopoly in the economy. When Amazon.com opened its website in 1995, Barnes and Noble followed in 1997 with BarnesandNoble.com. Such imitation also occurred between Border and Books-a-Million (see Dornbusch et al., 2004, p. 81).

Information flow

Firms continuously strive for information about technology, markets, and competition to improve their growth prospects and innovative processes (Porter, 1990, p. 638). The flow of information about buyers, sellers, and related industries, upstream and downstream, are provided regularly by trade associations such as Bowker and the Book Industry Study Group (BISG).

Joseph Stiglitz has expressed doubt as to the validity of supply and demand models to express information content. He points out that information is collected and processed on a continuous basis, and one must therefore have a model to represent that activity (Stiglitz, 1985, p. 23). The search procedure on the buyer side is an attempt to stay abreast of the flow of current information.

One can distinguish between imperfect information regarding the characteristics of goods, as under adverse selection cases, and characteristics of individual actions, as under moral hazard conditions. Hidden information in the principal-agent problems characterizes moral hazard cases in the book industry. Retailers act as agents for the publisher, who is the principal. For example, publishers may set prices and retailers buy at those prices and perhaps sell at a markup price. In these relationships the publisher has market power over prices, but may have to carry the burden of sales taxes. Hidden information also surfaces in adverse selection forms, such as a lemon problem in the book industry. Often, a person may not read enough to build enough human capital to maximize his lifetime returns. Also, a reader does not get to preview a book before purchase on the web. Imperfect information in those instances requires government intervention, so that the equilibrium is not optimal (Stiglitz, 1985, p. 27).

Imperfect information can be treated as a tax where low ability is subsidized and high ability is taxed (Stiglitz, 1985, p. 28). In our search example for the book industry, information is embedded in a distribution of prices. More information implies that the distribution of prices will change to make the agents better informed. The dispersion of prices will be affected by different policies of firms regarding tax and risk phenomena. In the end, one does not expect the outcome to be efficient (Stiglitz, 2009, p. 583).

One area of much difficulty is obtaining information about risks in the book industry. The most difficult part of risk analysis is associated with the state of the economy, such as when the economy slows down or grows. Such movements occur at random. The underlying risk associated with random movements in prices would create an expected price distribution. Information from surveys indicates that consumer confidence in the book industry fell during the Great Recession, which would result in a fall in demand and subsequent fall in prices. A recent report (A. C. Neilson, *Consumer Confidence Survey*—Q1 2010: Field dates March 8, 2010–March 28, 2010) indicates that consumer willingness to buy on the Internet slumped during the Great Recession. Two years before the recession, the confidence index on book purchases on the web increased by 7 percent, from 34 percent 2006 to 41 percent in 2008. Two years into the recession, the confidence index increased by only 3 percent, from 41 percent in 2008 to 44 percent in 2010. The difference-in-difference indicates that consumer confidence during the downturn fell by 4 percent, a devastating state-of-the-economy effect.

Information is provided even when the price of a book is zero: the case of Microsoft has taught us that a zero price for a product (Internet Explorer) is an attempt to block entry. This zero price strategy of booksellers on the Internet leads potential customers to search for a book on a particular site with a particular price distribution. When a book is offered for free on the web, no one will object to the fact that it will create the tendency for buyers to come again to that particular seller or site. But a fear is entertained that when the number of freebies becomes sufficiently large, buyers will hop around from site to site and perhaps saturate their reading capacity. What is lacking in such an argument is that by merely surfing around a large number of discrete sites, they will come closer and closer to some sites. Their search will eventually lead them to a convergent number of sites to which they would return. To use a somewhat mathematical term, a sort of Cauchy convergence on a series or sequence of searches is taking place, that is, discrete searches may lead buyers to take a closer look at some particular sites.

Some of the appropriate conclusions from the information side of the book market can be summarized. First, the standard market equilibrium ignores information even at a general equilibrium level (Stiglitz, 2009, p. ix). Adverse selection outcomes can take the form of reading enough to maintain the human capital level to perform on the job or not being able to preview a book before purchase. Third, similar books may be sold for different prices in different stores, depending on the principal-agent relationship. It is also a recognized fact that prices are dispersed on the Internet and a search procedure is necessary, probably because it is optimal for firms to charge different prices (Stiglitz, 1985, p. 29).

In summary, this chapter grapples with the demand and supply aspects of the book industry. The investigation is complex, with the demand side displaying components relating to consumption and human capital formation. The supply side features exogenous and endogenous information content that is incomplete. The two sides of the market come together not in an efficient way, but under condition of imperfect competition.

3
Consumption Aspects: Empirical Findings

Abstract: *Consumption is a driver of the book industry, and therefore impacts profits as the state of the economy changes. The overall state is that production rates are almost twice as large as consumption rates—but prices remain high, partly because they are traditionally cost-push in nature. The highest-cost aspects of the industry have traditionally been paper, platemaking, printing, binding, and book returns. Information technology is changing those costs as book production moves online or overseas. As a result, the industry has experienced some severe short-term business cycles that have been devastating to firms like Borders Books, which exited the industry in 2011. Our empirical study shows that price is elastic for all major book categories, indicating that price competition is still alive, though the industry also practices nonprice competition.*

Ramrattan, Lall, and Michael Szenberg. *Revolutions in Book Publishing: The Effects of Digital Innovation on the Industry.* New York: Palgrave Macmillan, 2016.
DOI: 10.1057/9781137576217.0008.

We looked at several indicators that underlie the consumption aspects of the publishing industry: quantity, sales, consumer expenditures, employment, and prices. Table 3.1 indicates these trends, ascertained by a regression of the log arithmetic of the variables on a constant and time trend. The results of Table 3.1 indicate that all the indicators' variables are growing over time, except employment. Special modeling was attempted to improve the Durbin-Watson statistics.

In the previous chapter we discussed the theoretical underpinnings of demand and the consumption aspect in the book industry. A demand side interpretation of the results in Table 3.1 indicates that as consumer expenditures increase 0.06 percent annually, unit sales rise at approximately 0.3, meeting approximately half the demand and increasing pressure on prices to rise. The matching supply indicates that publishers were overzealous in the amount of book output. Publishers produce 0.13 percent annually, while sales have expanded by less than half that number.

Overall price increases were at or slightly above inflation rates, and therefore indicate a balanced market. Prices for hardbacks and paperbacks matched the rise in demand. Approximately half the annual rates of price increases were due to inflation, as the CPI increased from 130.7 in 1990 to 179.9 in 2002 or 3.2 percent annually (Greco, 2005, p. 360).

Bracketing the growth rates in Table 3.1 are two extremes. At one extreme, Bowker data shows that book output increased at a rate of 0.13 percent annually from 1990 to 2008. At the other extreme, the employment trend decreased by approximately a 0.007 annual rate over the sample period. The following section addresses the first extreme. Employment declines will be analyzed in the next chapter under manpower and productivity.

Short-term perspective

Zeroing in on the 1999–2004 period, Paula Bernstein found the following short period conclusions: (1) bookstores' and publishers' revenues are subject to short-term fluctuations; (2) consumer expenditures were increasing; (3) unit sales were falling; and (4) overall prices have been rising, although hardback prices have been falling (Bernstein, 2005 pp. 40–52). That study correlated the coverage of the different data sources to form a coherent picture.

TABLE 3.1 Long-term trends in the book publishing industry

Variable	Sample	Constant	Time	R^2	DW	Special Adj.
Industry trends						
Consumer expenditure ($b) (NAICS 51113)	1990–2007	2.78 (48.11)	0.06 (13.16)	0.97	1.97	ARMA(1,1)
Units sold (b) (NAICS 51113)	1990–2008	0.59 (10.55)	0.03 (6.1)	0.88	1.97	ARMA(1,1)
Book output (Bowker Data) (b)	1990–2008	−3.75 (49.24)	0.13 (21.74)	0.97	2.0	None
Employment (ths.) (NAICS 51113)	1990–2008	4.54 (151.0)	−0.007 (3.68)	0.78	2.0	ARMA(1,3)
Sales (BISG Data) ($b) (NAICS 51113)	1991–2008	2.62 (152.75)	0.06 (13.16)	0.97	2.0	(ARMA(2,1)
Sales (Census Data) ($B) (NAICS 451211)		2.15 (38.34)	0.04 (9.18)	0.97	0.56	MA(1)
Prices (BISGSales/ BISGQn) (NAICS 51113) (USD)	1991–2008	1.99 (21.86)	0.03 (3.46)	0.80	1.82	ARMA(1,1)
Prices (Hardbacks) (USD) (Bowker Data: Stat. Abst.)	1990–2002	3.59 (31.39)	0.05 (3.60)	0.67	1.90	AR(1)
Price (Paperback) (USD) (Bowker Data: Stat. Abst.)	1990–2002	2.70 (36.04)	0.06 (6.75)	0.82	1.92	AR(1)
Price (Mass Media) (USD) (Bowker Data: Stat. Abst.)	1989–2002	1.56 (29.84)	0.02 (3.90)	0.58	0.43	None

Source: See Appendix A3.1 for Data, Sources, and Regression Output.

The traditional hypothesis for rising prices is cost-push. For the mid-1990s, transportation costs made up approximately 40 percent of the cost of books (Dennis, LaMay, and Pease, 1997, p. 15). For instance, Albert Greco reported that "costs escalated dramatically in the mid-1990s because of a surge in fine paper costs" (Greco, 1997, p. 133). Other cost-driven price increases were associated with plate making, printing, binding, and book returns for that period. Although publishers may sign multiyear contracts for paper supply, "much of the impact of rising or falling paper prices is borne by the publisher...printers can also make money (or lose it) by buying ahead and maintaining inventories of paper" (S&P Industry Survey: Publishing, April 21, 2008).

During the mid-1990s, firms embraced changes in computer and Internet technology, which impacted all aspects of the book publishing industry. Authors and editors use text editors and desktop publishing systems in their handling of manuscripts, text, and images, which has reduced costs in production, reprinting, and inventory management. This happened side-by-side with the advent of electronic book publishing, providing a constant cost scenario for small and large batch printing. Initial competition was very devastating for many firms on the Internet. Downsizing was rampant, and companies such as Audiohighway.com, Bookface.com, Booktech, and Contentville.com had to exit the market altogether. Companies were faced with the paradoxical choice of trading off short-term profit for a presence on the Web. This aspect will be treated more fully in the chapter on Internet in this book.

Initially, the idea was prevalent that the brick-and-mortar business of book publishing was on the way out. Thomas Mann, reference librarian at the Library of Congress, has argued against that idea, indicating that the digital medium is not an ideal way of preserving manuscripts (Mann, 2001, p. 273). From the inception of electronic books, Walt Crawford, former president of the Library and Information Technology Association, saw a coexistence of physical and electronic book forms when he wrote that

> Books matter, and will continue to matter, because people learn from them and enjoy reading them. Public and academic libraries will continue to rely heavily on printed collections because they work so well for the ideas of the future as well as the record of the past and present. Of course, libraries will extend those printed collections with in-house media collections, borrowed physical resources, and an ever-growing array of digital publications and online retrieval: that's neither revolutionary nor even new. (Crawford, 1998, p. 22)

Nevertheless, some analysts see the possibility of a fully electronic publishing landscape within the short-term horizon, perhaps in the next 20 years.

Price characteristics of demand for books

When the classical economist Alfred Marshall published his book *Industry and Trade*, he asked the publisher to lower the price in order to reach a larger audience. At issue was the cost of production for a run of 2,000 copies, which Marshall broke down as follows: composition and printing: £605, material and binding: £433, and advertising: £100, for a total of £1,138.

Marshall then requested "the price of 18s...if paper were not still rather dear...I should have liked an even lower price" (Marshall, 1996, 3:365). The publisher responded that "it is true that paper is going down slightly, but not to anything like pre-war process; and printing and binding, owing to the demand of the wage receivers, are if anything likely to go up" (ibid., p. 366).

Marshall considered his work precious and was willing to forgo profits from republications. He undoubtedly assumed that lower pricing would widen the market, showing the law of demand at work. However, he was also espousing a cost plus pricing mechanism.

As with US cars, new books come with a list price. Wholesalers buy books at a discount, which can be as high as 50 percent off the list price, and books that are warehoused for too long can be discounted to wholesalers by as much as 80 percent (Clerides, 2002, p. 1387). Books are sold mainly at their list price, contributing to price stability. But it is not hard to find "used and discounted new in-print books available through Abebooks, Amazon, and Alibris, many of them in large quantities and at heavy discounts from list price" (Levine-Clark, 2004, p. 296).

Marshall's simplistic model must be brought up to date: cost is still a concern. Printing and Publishing are often separate activities for manufacturers and are so globally. Consumer search cost, which is now facilitated by search engines on the Internet, would have to be a concern in modern pricing. Traditionally, by studying the nature of pricing, we should be able to infer structural characteristics of the firm. According to George Bittlingmayer, the market structure of the firm is monopolistic competition, a mixture of monopoly and competition. Under this market, we find many firms, each with some market power. Prices are not determined as in perfect competition, but at a point where demand intersects with average cost. Our approach to the market structure, however, would be empirical rather than theoretical. We begin with a transcendental logarithmic (translog) demand function for books, and then make some inferences about competition.

Translog demand for books

This section will examine the demand characteristics of the book publishing industry empirically. The empirical analysis is done from a disaggregated point of view across several categories—Adult Trade

(ADU), Book Club (BOC), College Books (COL), Elementary and High School Text (ELHI), Juvenile Trade Books (JUV), Mail Order Books (MAI), Mass Market Paperback (MMP), Professional Books (PRO), and Religious Books (REL).

For the sample period 1985–2002, we display the share of retail sales of these categories in Figure 3.1. The first group, with the highest shares, is made up of Adult Trade and Religious books. The second group, with the next largest shares, includes Elementary and High School Texts and College books. All the other categories make up the third group with the lowest share. Those categories' shares remained fairly stable over the sample period, except for professional books, whose share has declined steadily since 1991.

In the previous chapter, we indicated that a demand curve is underscored by a utility function, which can be simple or complex. Early studies of translog demand were skeptical about the function's ability to explain the reality of demand better than, say, a simple Cobb-Douglas form. Evidence to settle this skepticism was lacking as early studies were based on small sample sizes (Cramer, 1971, p. 253). However, the literature subsequently witnessed a proliferation of translog studies, mandating an examination of this demand form of specification for this study.

By Shepherd's rule and Roy's identity, we can regress the share of, say, retail sales on prices. The retail sales share of each category of books $i = 1 \ldots 9$ is derived from the equation: $Share_i = \partial Log\,(Sales) / \partial P_i$, (Greene, 2000, p. 642), which requires us to use a *numeraire* price to avoid singularity in estimation.

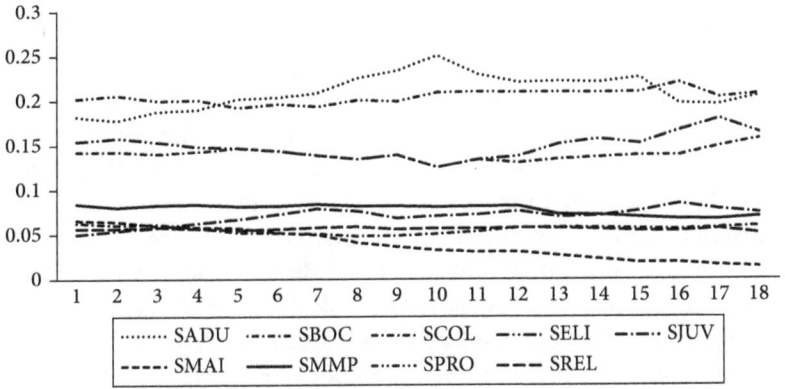

FIGURE 3.1   *Book category share, 1985–2002*

By restricting some of the parameters of the translog function, a number of tests can be performed. A favorite test, generally known as separability, is to see if some of the prices can be grouped together (Arrow, 1985, 5:458). This is interesting for our case, where the cross-price terms may have similar influences on the different categories of books. To test that, one can simply set the cross-price coefficient equal before performing the regression. Other restrictions, such as that the prices can be added, or that the utility function be homothetic, where a function of all the prices is homogenous to degree 1, do not seem relevant to our case, and are omitted in this investigation.

In scientific parlance, we are therefore leaning toward two hypotheses in this investigation. One hypothesis can be stated in the traditional way, namely, to assess whether sales are responsive to price changes, other things remaining the same. The other hypothesis is in the nature of competition among the various categories of books. To this second hypothesis, we can append subsidiary hypotheses to account for whether the industry is besieged by market power in pricing. A traditional measure of this market power is the Lerner index, which ascertains whether substitution between book categories is occurring.

To examine the translog demand function, we obtained prices from the retail sales of the earlier-mentioned categories of books, by dividing the sales for each book category by its respective quantity. The specification we examined use the price of Religious Books as the *numeraire*, yielding a set of relative prices for the independent variables: {padu/prel, pboc/prel, pcol/prel, peli/prel, pjuv/prel, pmai/prel, pmmp/prel, ppro/prel}, to explain a set of dependent variables: {sadu, sboc, scol, seli, sjuv, smai, smmp, spro}. In these relationships, the prefixes "S" and "P" indicate sales and price data, respectively, and the model is fitted in log form.

The results of the translog regressions are given in Table 3.2. For the nonseparable case, the results are weakest for the Juvenile book category, where the t-values are mostly insignificant. Other nonsignificant relations indicate that the price of elementary and high school (ELHI) and professional books does not affect the share of Adult Trade books; the price of Adult books does not affect the share of Book Clubs books; the price of juvenile and professional book does not affect the share of ELHI; the price of college books does not affect the share of mass media paperbacks, and the price of book club books does not affect the price

TABLE 3.2 Translog regression: nonseparable results, 1985–2002

	Adult trade	Book clubs	College	ELHI	Juvenile	Mail order	Mass media	Professional
Constant	−3.02 (−7.33)***	−4.48 (−8.95)***	0.97 (2.76)***	−3.15 (−5.77)***	−3.39 (−2.73)***	10.93 (9.131)***	1.64 (4.49)***	−4.72 (−16.64)***
Padu/Prel	1.64 (5.83)***	−0.15 (−0.48)	−1.79 (−7.66)*	−2.13 (−6.02)***	0.43 (0.49)	−3.85 (−4.95)***	0.64 (2.81)***	1.15 (6.38)***
Pboc/Prel	−2.00 (−9.68)***	2.35 (9.11)***	1.14 (6.39)***	0.71 (2.55)***	0.60 (0.79)	4.13 (6.79)***	0.63 (3.45)***	−0.12 (−0.84)
Pcol/Prel	0.32 (2.49)***	−0.94 (−6.11)***	0.79 (7.72)***	−0.59 (−3.48)***	−0.32 (−1.69)*	1.86 (4.96)***	0.66 (−5.98)	−0.51 (−6.29)***
Peli/Prel	0.37 (−1.54)	0.72 (2.53)***	−1.81 (−9.44)***	0.60 (1.94)**	0.57 (1.11)	−6.58 (−9.63)***	−1.64 (−8.13)***	1.30 (8.50)***
Pjuv/Prel	−0.44 (−4.43)***	−0.40 (−3.45)***	0.68 (8.15)***	0.88 (−6.82)	−0.08 (−0.19)	1.03 (3.63)***	−0.64 (−7.64)***	−0.39 (−5.81)***
Pmai/Prel	−0.50 (−2.96)***	1.07 (5.44)***	−0.64 (−4.48)***	−0.65 (−3.01)***	0.72 (1.63)*	2.43 (5.10)***	0.79 (5.66)***	0.55 (4.98)***
Pmmp/Prel	−0.21 (−0.77)	−1.13 (−3.51)***	1.37 (6.00)***	0.18 (0.50)	−1.17 (−1.87)*	2.59 (3.32)***	1.08 (4.75)***	−1.63 (−8.92)***
Ppro/Prel	0.34 (−1.24)	0.65 (1.97)**	−0.94 (−4.06)***	1.85 (5.14)***4	−0.14 (−0.20)	−7.43 (−9.46)***	−2.81 (−11.56)***	1.02 (5.67)***
R²	0.97	0.93	0.93	0.94	0.84	0.99	0.96	0.90
D.W.	2.34	1.89	2.97	2.72	1.55	2.08	2.82	2.94

Note: The significant levels are: * = 90 percent level, ** = 95 percent level, *** = 99 percent level.

of professional books. We notice that college and mail order books are affected by all the relative prices.

Because of the singularity restriction we placed on the model, namely, using the prices of religious books as a *numeraire*, we have to estimate the coefficients of the religious books category and calculate their own elasticities of prices. The latter is achieved by the formula:

$$(coef \cdot_{ii} + share_i(share_i - 1)) / share_i^2 = coef \cdot_{ii} / share_i + share_i - 1$$

The results of Table 3.3 indicate elastic responses to price cuts for all book categories and low profit margins. Own price elasticity varies for each sample point of the data from 1985 to 2002.

We need to take into consideration that modern innovations started in the 1990s, about the central years of the data points. Often, innovation follows the creative destruction path advocated by Joseph Schumpeter, who argued that "[t]he fundamental impulse that sets and keeps the capitalist engine in motion comes from the new consumers' goods, the new methods of production or transportation, the new markets...This process of Creative Destruction is the essential fact about capitalism" (Schumpteter, 1942, p. 83). Another theory is the life cycle hypothesis proposed in the mid-1960s by Raymond Vernon. The essential point is that innovation operates in phases as information is diffused in the economy and globally. We therefore present elasticity estimates in Table 3.3, and for the average share in the sample period in Table 3.4.

The striking overall observation of Table 3.3 is that for all book categories, the response of sales to price changes is elastic. Not only is the elasticity greater than 1, but the measures range mostly from −2 to −4. For the sample period, elasticity remained fairly stable for all categories except mail order books (OMAI), for which elasticity had been escalating since 1999. Mail Order is the category of books with the least market share, and had been losing share most rapidly as indicated in Figure 3.1. This could have prompted price cuts in order to sell more.

Overall, the book publishing industry has been robust and open to innovation, in that the overall level of the price elasticity has not been changing for the book categories. Periods 1 and 2 in Table 3.4 represent the time before and after Internet technology was revolutionizing the industry. The average elasticity mostly declined during the second period, except for Mail Order and Religious books. Apparently the proliferation of electronic gadgets is a good and viable substitute for reading, so that

TABLE 3.3 Own elasticity by book categories estimated from regression results

Year	OBOC	OCOL	OELI	OJUV	OMAI	OMMP	OPRO	OREL	OSADU
1985	−3.71	−2.03	−1.73	−4.14	−2.30	−3.73	−3.32	−2.47	−3.67
1986	−3.75	−2.03	−1.69	−4.07	−2.34	−3.78	−3.31	−2.46	−3.68
1987	−3.74	−2.05	−1.74	−4.01	−2.46	−3.75	−3.33	−2.43	−3.65
1988	−3.80	−2.03	−1.79	−3.93	−2.50	−3.74	−3.32	−2.47	−3.65
1989	−3.90	−1.98	−1.81	−3.87	−2.52	−3.77	−3.35	−2.51	−3.63
1990	−3.92	−2.02	−1.84	−3.79	−2.66	−3.76	−3.34	−2.48	−3.62
1991	−3.93	−2.07	−1.90	−3.71	−2.72	−3.74	−3.34	−2.43	−3.62
1992	−3.99	−2.11	−1.95	−3.74	−3.00	−3.76	−3.32	−2.41	−3.59
1993	−3.98	−2.07	−1.89	−3.85	−3.17	−3.76	−3.33	−2.48	−3.58
1994	−3.93	−2.22	−2.06	−3.82	−3.31	−3.77	−3.30	−2.46	−3.57
1995	−3.89	−2.12	−1.95	−3.80	−3.39	−3.76	−3.30	−2.47	−3.59
1996	−3.81	−2.16	−1.91	−3.75	−3.39	−3.76	−3.30	−2.44	−3.60
1997	−3.80	−2.11	−1.76	−3.83	−3.58	−3.87	−3.30	−2.45	−3.60
1998	−3.81	−2.09	−1.70	−3.82	−3.80	−3.88	−3.30	−2.48	−3.60
1999	−3.82	−2.07	−1.75	−3.75	−4.04	−3.91	−3.30	−2.53	−3.59
2000	−3.84	−2.07	−1.61	−3.65	−4.02	−3.94	−3.28	−2.55	−3.64
2001	−3.81	−1.96	−1.48	−3.72	−4.27	−3.95	−3.32	−2.48	−3.64
2002	−3.78	−1.88	−1.63	−3.77	−4.42	−3.91	−3.31	−2.62	−3.62
Average	−3.84	−2.06	−1.79	−3.83	−3.22	−3.81	−3.31	−2.48	−3.62

Source: Estimated are from Regression Results, using the formula: $\left(\dfrac{coef_{ii}}{share_i}\right) + share_i - 1$.

TABLE 3.4 Own elasticity and Lerner power index based on regression results

	Average elasticities			Period 1 versus 2	
	Own elasticity	Period 1 1985–1995	Period 2 1996–2002	% change	Lerner index
Book club	−3.84	−3.87	−3.81	−1.53	0.26
College text	−2.06	−2.07	−2.05	−0.84	0.49
ELHI	−1.79	−1.85	−1.69	−8.55	0.56
Juvenile	−3.83	−3.88	−3.76	−3.31	0.26
Mail order	−3.22	−2.76	−3.93	42.37	0.31
Mass media	−3.81	−3.76	−3.89	3.53	0.26
Professional	−3.31	−3.32	−3.30	−0.71	0.30
Religious	−2.48	−2.46	−2.51	1.84	0.40
Adult trade	−3.62	−3.62	−3.61	−0.31	0.28

people do not respond as before to a price cut. In addition, price cutting on the Internet is apparently not a viable rivalry weapon for firms, since the proliferation of search engines makes it easy to imitate a price cut. This would imply that firms would be willing to cooperate on price policy, and venture more into nonprice competition, such as in services or shipping.

The last column of Table 3.4 displays the Lerner index to capture market power, if any, by displaying the percent difference between price and marginal costs. The values range from 0.26 for Book Clubs to 0.56 for ELHI, suggesting some market power in setting book price. Although a book comes with a list price, which is set by the publisher, the prices we use in the analysis are retail prices, and therefore do not reflect the sizable discounts usually obtained by booksellers.

In this chapter on consumption, we find that demand for books during the sample period remained healthy, and elasticity shows some weakening from substitution of electronic gadgets for reading time. High elasticity in the book publishing business is not necessarily a consequence of price wars among sellers, as such price cuts are easily recognized via search engines and can therefore be imitated. One suggestion of this finding is that firms may prefer nonprice rivalry and price collusion. We also noticed that prices are not significantly out of line with inflation rates, placing growth in the industry on a productivity foundation.

The results are not at variance with long-term expansion of book production. Elasticity of demand remains high in the face of some decline. The revenue share of the different categories of books is holding steady, except for professional books, whose share has been declining since 1991. The price-marginal cost margin, as measured by the Lerner index, indicates some market power in the industry.

The sample we used did not extend into the recent deep recession scenario. In the prerecession phase, Bowker data shows that book output expanded by 0.13 percent annually from 1990 to 2008. As expected during a recession, the employment trend decreased at an approximately 0.007 annual rate over the sample period.

Appendix

Data definitions and sources

1 Quantity data.

The quantity data reported in various years of the Statistical Abstract of the United States lists its source as the Book Industry Study Group, Inc (BISG), New York, *Book Industry Trend*, Annual Data. This data is reported in Table 3A.2 as QNBISG (in Billions).

Table 3A.2 also reports book output data from R. R. Bowker. This data is available in Greco's 1997 and 2005 books, for the years up to 2001. More current data is taken from various Bowker press releases found at: http://www.bowker.com/index.php/press-releases-2006. A characteristic of this data is that it does not count data from backlisted titles, which are older titles that continue to be printed and sold.

2 Sales data

We have several sources for sales and revenue data as well, including US Census data for 1992–present, with sources listed in Table A3.1. Sales data for BISG is provided side-by-side with the Census data in Table A3.2.

3 Price data

Price data for hardbacks, paperbacks, and mass market books are taken from various years from the Statistical Abstract of the United States. The Statistical Abstract acknowledges that the data comes from R. R. Bowker. The series is consistent only up to 2002, as listed in Table A3.3.

4 Labor input data

The Bureau of Labor and Statistics provides Nonfarm Wage and Salary employment data, which we display in Table A3-2. The data is extracted from the agency web site using the following inputs: Series Id: CEU5051113001, Not Seasonally Adjusted, Super Sector: Information, Industry: Book publishers, NAICS Code: 51113, Data Type: All Employees, thousands. BLS also provides data on the unemployment rate—TableA 3.1, and hours worked—TableA3.2. Additional employment data is provided by the Statistical Abstract of the United States.

5 Capital

Capital is not directly observed. One estimate can be derived by adding up notes and accounts receivable, inventory, and depreciable assets for the NAICS 51113, which we took from the S&P Compustat Tapes. An alternative is to use the Physical Plant and Equipment for that NAICS code, which we took from the Mergent business database.

6 Consumer expenditures

Domestic Consumer Expenditure is reported in various issues of the Statistical Abstract of the United States. The 2009 Statistical Abstract notes that the source of the data is the Book Industry Study Group: Book Industry Trends, 2008, Annual.

TABLE 3A.1 US book stores (NAICS 451211) sales, 2000–current ($m)

Year	January	February	March	April	May	June	July	August	September	October	November	December	Total	% change
1992	790	540	536	524	553	589	593	895	863	647	642	1,166	8,338	–
1993	999	568	602	583	613	619	608	985	905	669	693	1,275	9,119	9.37
1994	1,055	636	635	610	684	726	679	1,156	1,023	733	772	1,410	10,119	10.97
1995	1,309	720	696	689	786	808	783	1,248	1,103	747	851	1,468	11,208	10.76
1996	1,375	758	743	751	855	839	787	1,361	1,042	899	908	1,600	11,918	6.33
1997	1,559	825	813	806	893	876	830	1,301	1,159	926	996	1,771	12,755	7.02
1998	1,467	923	883	854	920	939	882	1,385	1,247	954	991	1,849	13,294	4.23
1999	1,514	990	976	934	977	1,032	1,024	1,388	1,242	1,020	1,090	1,998	14,185	6.70
2000	1,506	1,091	1,031	975	1,105	1,123	1,049	1,595	1,407	1,015	1,100	1,895	14,892	4.98
2001	1,586	1,070	1,063	935	1,071	1,078	1,006	1,821	1,407	1,016	1,099	1,958	15,110	1.46
2002	1,973	1,001	1,009	968	1,118	1,046	1,038	1,799	1,491	998	1,060	1,949	15,450	2.25
2003	2,056	990	923	974	1,105	1,178	1,125	2,132	1,567	1,042	1,032	2,055	16,179	4.72
2004	2,135	1,099	1,064	1,014	1,102	1,196	1,161	2,101	1,549	1,063	1,083	2,190	16,757	3.57
2005	2,066	1,081	1,094	992	1,113	1,146	1,205	2,202	1,540	1,053	1,137	2,232	16,861	0.62
2006	2,198	1,085	1,075	972	1,157	1,219	1,117	2,107	1,532	1,043	1,126	2,102	16,733	–0.76
2007	2,195	1,030	1,019	926	1,125	1,152	1,213	2,311	1,564	1,123	1,211	2,152	17,021	5.20
2008	2,271	1,139	1,012	994	1,141	1,065	1,115	2,402	1,476	1,044	1,046	2,039	16,744	–1.63
2009	2,233	1,010	998	969	5,210	5,416								

Source: http://www.census.gov/mrts/www/data/delimited/nsalo9.dat.

TABLE 3A.2 Time series data for the book publishing industry

Year	QNBISG (b)	SALESBISG ($b)	SALESCEN ($b)	CONEXPEN ($b)	EMPALL (ths.)	Pub. rev. ($b)	Output Bowker (ths.)
1989	2.00	14.11	NA	18.04	NA	14.111	NA
1990	2.01	14.86	NA	19.04	85.60	14.983	27.93
1991	2.04	15.57	NA	20.10	83.50	15.702	27.73
1992	2.05	16.33	8.34	21.22	82.00	16.470	49.28
1993	2.08	17.39	9.12	22.63	82.40	17.541	46.19
1994	2.13	18.18	10.12	23.91	84.00	18.405	51.86
1995	2.19	19.49	11.21	25.15	85.70	19.471	62.04
1996	2.22	20.15	11.92	26.15	87.60	20.286	68.18
1997	2.18	20.97	12.76	27.02	89.20	21.132	61.70
1998	2.40	22.34	13.29	28.79	88.60	22.507	119.26
1999	2.51	23.76	14.19	30.03	87.20	23.482	120.24
2000	2.46	24.58	14.89	36.14	88.30	NA	122.11
2001	2.36	24.56	15.11	36.06	87.50	NA	141.70
2002	2.37	26.78	15.45	36.80	83.40	NA	150.00
2003	2.34	27.82	16.18	37.91	78.80	NA	175.00
2004	2.97	28.85	16.76	39.20	81.80	NA	195.00
2005	3.08	28.03	16.86	51.92	82.40	NA	282.50
2006	3.10	28.19	16.73	54.24	82.60	NA	274.42
2007	3.13	37.26	17.02	56.63	81.50	NA	284.37
2008	3.10	43.32	16.74	NA	80.20	NA	275.23

TABLE 3A.3 Historic trade trend data 1992–2006 (sths.), paper and publishing products

	1992	1993	1994	1995	1996	1997	1998	1999	2000	2001	2002	2003	2004	2005	2006
Australia	273	296	353	429	496	527	379	516	551	578	581	802	868	958	981
New Zealand	466	471	572	717	695	579	555	588	724	698	612	675	830	942	929
Hong Kong	1,177	1,056	1,063	1,158	1,121	1,083	939	833	943	781	784	1,359	1,496	1,568	1,630
China	465	890	1,107	1,620	1,516	1,725	1,868	2,167	2,969	3,243	3,592	2,849	4,252	4,643	6,328
Korea	471	715	893	1,266	1,368	1,541	1,831	1,886	2,032	2,108	1,869	2,231	2,681	2,698	2,755
Taiwan	759	1,004	734	846	854	792	800	738	746	893	996	1,153	1,378	1,330	1,431
Southeast Asia	1,446	1,818	2,345	3,551	3,273	3,444	4,540	5,055	6,011	5,954	5,759	6,620	7,410	8,085	8,857
India	52	62	115	172	136	127	147	194	265	292	364	491	499	641	721
Canada	12,451	12,214	13,871	20,355	16,965	16,429	16,140	16,894	19,965	18,356	16,942	17,305	19,082	19,933	20,239
United States	14,002	13,686	15,567	20,573	18,859	19,064	18,496	18,496	20,380	19,279	18,172	20,378	22,110	23,626	25,460
Mexico	301	294	368	690	670	805	893	919	1,029	1,013	1,093	1,119	1,265	1,568	1,680
Argentina	108	126	174	404	368	372	409	329	393	361	320	393	492	490	578
Brazil	1,566	1,602	2,023	2,742	2,115	2,110	2,083	2,282	2,718	2,438	2,435	3,220	3,629	4,214	5,046
Latin America	982	1,056	1,408	2,137	1,646	1,675	1,663	1,661	2,165	2,236	2,016	2,232	2,625	2,997	3,225
EU_25	60,500	52,876	62,368	82,467	76,232	73,041	75,720	74,875	75,643	75,694	79,006	92,654	103,393	106,574	114,667
MENA	402	435	537	689	574	616	750	776	842	920	956	1,391	1,467	1,912	1,990
South Africa	734	728	746	1,088	828	792	856	835	1,137	1,048	791	1,370	1,221	1,322	1,335
Russia	376	514	697	1,740	1,613	1,689	1,539	1,540	2,236	2,195	2,141	2,372	2,593	2,886	3,068
RoW	2,203	1,884	2,246	2,903	2,841	2,783	3,097	3,003	3,225	3,475	3,535	4,788	5,529	6,086	5,733
Total	100,964	94,182	109,736	148,403	134,513	131,678	135,054	136,231	146,958	144,162	144,758	166,591	186,587	196,437	210,654

Source: Compiled from GTAP 7 Time Series Data Base.

TABLE 3A.4 *Hardback, paperback, and mass media prices*

	PRICEHARD	PRICEMASS	PRICEPAP
1989	40.61000	4.320000	17.16000
1990	42.12000	4.570000	17.45000
1991	44.17000	5.080000	18.40000
1992	45.05000	5.220000	18.81000
1993	34.98000	5.820000	20.56000
1994	44.65000	5.700000	20.56000
1995	47.15000	6.530000	21.71000
1996	50.00000	6.570000	21.41000
1997	72.67000	6.340000	22.56000
1998	63.53000	NA	22.86000
1999	62.32000	5.640000	32.93000
2000	60.84000	5.770000	31.07000
2001	70.05000	6.310000	38.20000
2002	59.80000	6.480000	29.42000
2003	NA	NA	NA
2004	NA	NA	NA
2005	NA	NA	NA
2006	NA	NA	NA
2007	NA	NA	NA
2008	NA	NA	NA

Source: Bowker Data as reported in several issues of the Statistical Abstract of the United States The 1998 observation for mass media prices were left out for it appears anomalous to the series at approximately $9.

TABLE 3A.5 *Regression analysis of growth trends*

Dependent Variable: LOG(SALESBISG)
Method: Least Squares
Date: 07/16/09   Time: 18:43
Sample(adjusted): 1991 2008
Included observations: 18 after adjusting endpoints
Convergence achieved after 8 iterations
Backcast: 1990

Variable	Coefficient	Std. Error	t-Statistic	Prob.
C	2.618655	0.017143	152.7547	0.0000
TIME	0.046846	0.001530	30.62110	0.0000
AR(2)	−1.245731	0.423876	−2.938905	0.0108
MA(1)	0.558425	0.237420	2.352052	0.0338

Dependent Variable: LOG(CONEXPEN)
Method: Least Squares
Date: 07/16/09 Time: 18:30
Sample(adjusted): 1990 2007
Included observations: 18 after adjusting endpoints
Convergence achieved after 14 iterations
Backcast: 1989

Variable	Coefficient	Std. error	t-statistic	Prob.
C	2.775845	0.057695	48.11263	0.0000
TIME	0.063252	0.004805	13.16369	0.0000
AR(1)	0.286143	0.606357	0.471905	0.6443
MA(1)	0.168358	0.612672	0.274793	0.7875
R-squared	0.973450	Mean dependent var		3.439179
Adjusted R-squared	0.967761	S.D. dependent var		0.338325
S.E. of regression	0.060747	Akaike info criterion		−2.571070
Sum squared resid	0.051663	Schwarz criterion		−2.373210
Log likelihood	27.13963	F-statistic		171.1040
Durbin-Watson stat	1.971072	Prob(F-statistic)		0.000000

Dependent Variable: LOG(QNBISG)
Method: Least Squares
Date: 07/16/09 Time: 18:23
Sample(adjusted): 1990 2008
Included observations: 19 after adjusting endpoints
Convergence achieved after 17 iterations
Backcast: 1989

Variable	Coefficient	Std. error	t-statistic	Prob.
C	0.593292	0.056244	10.54848	0.0000
TIME	0.026542	0.004353	6.096965	0.0000
AR(1)	0.327277	0.407360	0.803410	0.4343

MA(1)	0.283301	0.425453	0.665880	0.5156
R-squared	0.901636	Mean dependent var	0.886956
Adjusted R-squared	0.881964	S.D. dependent var	0.158308
S.E. of regression	0.054389	Akaike info criterion	−2.800652
Sum squared resid	0.044372	Schwarz criterion	−2.601822
Log likelihood	30.60619	F-statistic	45.83183
Durbin-Watson stat	1.971409	Prob(F-statistic)	0.000000

Dependent Variable: LOG(EMPALL)
Method: Least Squares
Date: 07/16/09 Time: 18:13
Sample(adjusted): 1991 2008
Included observations: 18 after adjusting endpoints
Convergence achieved after 16 iterations
Backcast: 1988 1990

Variable	Coefficient	Std. error	t-statistic	Prob.
C	4.539252	0.030069	150.9615	0.0000
TIME	−0.007293	0.001980	−3.683387	0.0025
AR(1)	0.452693	0.199624	2.267730	0.0397
MA(3)	−0.931911	0.037148	−25.08620	0.0000
R-squared	0.778684	Mean dependent var		4.433264
Adjusted R-squared	0.731259	S.D. dependent var		0.037255
S.E. of regression	0.019313	Akaike info criterion		−4.862921
Sum squared resid	0.005222	Schwarz criterion		−4.665061
Log likelihood	47.76629	F-statistic		16.41931
Durbin-Watson stat	2.082162	Prob(F-statistic)		0.000073

Dependent Variable: LOG(SALES)
Method: Least Squares
Date: 06/23/09 Time: 10:41
Sample: 1992 2008
Included observations: 17

Variable	Coefficient	Std. error	t-statistic	Prob.
C	9.132275	0.039633	230.4200	0.0000
TIME	0.042934	0.003868	11.10038	0.0000
R-squared	0.891476	Mean dependent var		9.518682
Adjusted R-squared	0.884241	S.D. dependent var		0.229624
S.E. of regression	0.078126	Akaike info criterion		−2.150863
Sum squared resid	0.091555	Schwarz criterion		−2.052838
Log likelihood	20.28233	F-statistic		123.2185
Durbin-Watson stat	0.211143	Prob(F-statistic)		0.000000

Dependent Variable: LOG(SALESBISG/QNBISG)
Method: Least Squares
Date: 07/17/09 Time: 08:26
Sample(adjusted): 1990 2008
Included observations: 19 after adjusting endpoints
Convergence achieved after 13 iterations
Backcast: 1989

Variable	Coefficient	Std. error	t-statistic	Prob.
C	1.985993	0.090838	21.86303	0.0000
TIME	0.025204	0.007276	3.463884	0.0035
AR(1)	0.297411	0.440695	0.674868	0.5100
MA(1)	0.538422	0.375925	1.432258	0.1726
R-squared	0.802092	Mean dependent var		2.256232
Adjusted R-squared	0.762510	S.D. dependent var		0.161918
S.E. of regression	0.078907	Akaike info criterion		−2.056422
Sum squared resid	0.093395	Schwarz criterion		−1.857593
Log likelihood	23.53601	F-statistic		20.26423
Durbin-Watson stat	1.815988	Prob(F-statistic)		0.000016

Dependent Variable: LOG(PRICEHARD)
Method: Least Squares
Date: 07/17/09 Time: 08:34
Sample(adjusted): 1990 2002
Included observations: 13 after adjusting endpoints
Convergence achieved after 3 iterations

Variable	Coefficient	Std. error	t-statistic	Prob.
C	3.588966	0.114339	31.38868	0.0000
TIME	0.045895	0.012763	3.595944	0.0049
AR(1)	0.172999	0.330830	0.522923	0.6124
R-squared	0.667627	Mean dependent var		3.959501
Adjusted R-squared	0.601152	S.D. dependent var		0.223631
S.E. of regression	0.141233	Akaike info criterion		−0.877637
Sum squared resid	0.199468	Schwarz criterion		−0.747264
Log likelihood	8.704639	F-statistic		10.04332
Durbin-Watson stat	1.893296	Prob(F-statistic)		0.004056

Dependent Variable: LOG(PRICEPAP)
Method: Least Squares
Date: 07/17/09 Time: 08:42
Sample(adjusted): 1990 2002
Included observations: 13 after adjusting endpoints
Convergence achieved after 2 iterations

Variable	Coefficient	Std. error	t-statistic	Prob.
C	2.701496	0.074957	36.04058	0.0000
TIME	0.057439	0.008506	6.752381	0.0001
AR(1)	0.009626	0.332851	0.028919	0.9775

R-squared	0.824013	Mean dependent var		3.161162
Adjusted R-squared	0.788815	S.D. dependent var		0.246511
S.E. of regression	0.113284	Akaike info criterion		−1.318669
Sum squared resid	0.128332	Schwarz criterion		−1.188296
Log likelihood	11.57135	F-statistic		23.41117
Durbin-Watson stat	1.921487	Prob(F-statistic)		0.000169

Dependent Variable: LOG(PRICEMASS)
Method: Least Squares
Date: 07/17/09 Time: 09:10
Sample(adjusted): 1989 2002
Included observations: 13
Excluded observations: 1 after adjusting endpoints

Variable	Coefficient	Std. error	t-statistic	Prob.
C	1.558344	0.052212	29.84673	0.0000
TIME	0.024243	0.006223	3.895458	0.0025
R-squared	0.579745	Mean dependent var		1.735504
Adjusted R-squared	0.541540	S.D. dependent var		0.136567
S.E. of regression	0.092469	Akaike info criterion		−1.783245
Sum squared resid	0.094056	Schwarz criterion		−1.696329
Log likelihood	13.59109	F-statistic		15.17459
Durbin-Watson stat	0.432144	Prob(F-statistic)		0.002496

Dependent Variable: LOG(QNBISG)
Method: Least Squares
Date: 07/15/09 Time: 15:30
Sample(adjusted): 1991 2008
Included observations: 18 after adjusting endpoints
Convergence achieved after 28 iterations
Backcast: 1990

Variable	Coefficient	Std. error	t-statistic	Prob.
C	−3.898345	2.941743	−1.325182	0.2079
LOG(EMPALL)	1.000208	0.658036	1.519989	0.1525
TIME	0.031156	0.007764	4.012803	0.0015
AR(1)	0.547043	0.310274	1.763094	0.1014
MA(1)	0.334247	0.362361	0.922414	0.3731
R-squared	0.902851	Mean dependent var		0.897585
Adjusted R-squared	0.872959	S.D. dependent var		0.155766
S.E. of regression	0.055519	Akaike info criterion		−2.714042
Sum squared resid	0.040071	Schwarz criterion		−2.466717
Log likelihood	29.42638	F-statistic		30.20385
Durbin-Watson stat	1.968831	Prob(F-statistic)		0.000002
Inverted AR Roots	.55			
Inverted MA Roots	−.33			

Dependent Variable: LOG(OUTBOWKER/1000)
Method: Least Squares
Date: 07/21/09 Time: 16:28
Sample(adjusted): 1990 2008
Included observations: 19 after adjusting endpoints

Variable	Coefficient	Std. error	t-statistic	Prob.
C	−3.754966	0.076261	−49.23840	0.0000
TIME	0.134949	0.006206	21.74483	0.0000
R-squared	0.965295	Mean dependent var		−2.270527
Adjusted R-squared	0.963253	S.D. dependent var		0.772931
S.E. of regression	0.148167	Akaike info criterion		−0.881655
Sum squared resid	0.373208	Schwarz criterion		−0.782240
Log likelihood	10.37572	F-statistic		472.8377
Durbin-Watson stat	1.997898	Prob(F-statistic)		0.000000

Dependent Variable: LOG(SALESCEN)
Method: Least Squares
Date: 07/22/09 Time: 10:55
Sample(adjusted): 1992 2008
Included observations: 17 after adjusting endpoints
Convergence achieved after 7 iterations
Backcast: 1991

Variable	Coefficient	Std. error	t-statistic	Prob.
C	2.152234	0.056135	38.34056	0.0000
TIME	0.038408	0.004186	9.175614	0.0000
MA(1)	0.930390	0.025876	35.95549	0.0000
R-squared	0.968220	Mean dependent var		2.610405
Adjusted R-squared	0.963680	S.D. dependent var		0.229113
S.E. of regression	0.043664	Akaike info criterion		−3.265812
Sum squared resid	0.026691	Schwarz criterion		−3.118775
Log likelihood	30.75940	F-statistic		213.2657
Durbin-Watson stat	0.558799	Prob(F-statistic)		0.000000

Consumption Aspects: Empirical Findings   71

TABLE 3A.6   Book by book categories, 1985–2002 ($m)

Year	1 Adult	2 Juvenile	3 Religious	4 Professional	5 Book clubs	6 ELHI	7 College text	8 Mail order	9 MMP
1985	360	193	134	110	130	234	110	121	382
1986	352	210	133	117	126	228	111	124	381
1987	357	220	128	120	121	207	119	128	391
1988	365	244	121	125	112	202	130	138	419
1989	404	281	124	128	109	213	136	152	441
1990	403	301	130	131	108	209	137	138	433
1991	412	326	135	130	109	206	133	132	443
1992	442	319	140	135	106	208	137	110	439
1993	463	299	139	137	111	225	135	102	452
1994	492	320	142	142	116	211	136	96	461
1995	465	348	148	146	123	237	142	92	470
1996	446	370	154	144	132	247	150	93	467
1997	457	334	157	146	134	280	154	83	419
1998	476	355	161	150	138	291	161	76	429
1999	529	406	174	178	146	305	176	78	485
2000	564	592	133	187	112	152	83	68	421
2001	546	535	136	169	112	159	86	58	407
2002	550	539	138	170	113	162	88	55	411
2003	536	535	138	171	112	161	89	56	406

TABLE 3A.7   Revenues of book categories, 1985–2002: $m From Greco book

	Adult	Juvenile	Religious	Professional	Book clubs	ELHI	College text	Mail order	MMP
1985	1,735.3	475.6	536.7	1,928	598	1,472.9	1,358.4	629.6	803.7
1986	1,794.2	546.4	572.7	2,076.5	608.2	1,595.1	1,436.1	650.4	809.3
1987	2,077.7	635.1	638.8	2,207.3	678.7	1,695.8	1,549.5	657.6	913.7
1988	2,285.2	751.2	675.9	2,411.9	690.2	1,783.8	1,716.8	697.7	1,006.9
1989	2,722	901.5	737.1	2,592.8	704	1,983.6	1,983.6	768.8	1,094.5
1990	2,871.7	1,021.1	788	2,765.9	725.1	2,025.8	2,025.6	731.4	1,148.6
1991	3,088.8	1,163.8	854.7	2,860.7	749.8	2,054.2	2,054.2	733.6	1,243.9
1992	3,484.2	1,177.4	907.1	3,106.7	742.3	2,080.9	2,080.9	630.2	1,263.8
1993	3,887.2	1,136.1	931.5	3,320.5	804.7	2,318.1	2,318.1	601.2	1,359.4
1994	4,324.2	1,216.4	979.4	3,606.1	873.9	2,155.8	2,155.8	557.3	1,392.4
1995	4,234.1	1,326.7	1,036.8	3,869.3	976.1	2,466.2	2,466.2	559.5	1,499.6
1996	4,195.4	1,447.7	1,093.4	3,985	1,091.8	2,618	2,485.8	579.5	1,551.1
1997	4,395.3	1,378.8	1,132.7	4,156.4	1,143.1	3,005.4	2,669.7	521	1,433.8
1998	4,659.8	1,489.1	1,178	4,418.7	1,209.4	3,315	2,888.6	470	1,514.1
1999	5,083.9	1,708.2	1,216.9	4,720.4	1,272	3,424.7	3,128.8	412.8	1,552
2000	4,586.6	1,954.2	1,246.9	5,129.5	1,291.6	3,881.2	3,237.1	431.8	1,559.2
2001	4,553.7	1,816.2	1,305.1	4,739.1	1,334.5	4,183.6	3,468.9	353.9	1,546.6
2002	5,096.3	1,833.5	1,262.2	5,140.1	1,463.2	4,073.3	3,898.2	333.5	1,726.8

4
Production Aspects: Employment, Manpower, and Productivity

Abstract: *Production aspects of the book industry are in a state of perpetual mobility, with printed books facing strong competition from virtual space, Print on Demand (PoD), and e-books technologies. Our empirical analysis attempts to reconcile contrary views about increasing and constant returns to scale, using generally available data and standard econometric techniques. We embrace both the simple Cobb-Douglas and CES models of production. The Cobb-Douglas model indicates constant returns with weak statistical results, while the CES model indicates increasing returns. The overall results are subject to wide interpretation, underscoring a monopolistic structure, or a bilateral monopolistic model. The results also reached with modern discussion of increasing returns, which is normally sourced to the socialization of modern technological advances.*

Ramrattan, Lall, and Michael Szenberg. *Revolutions in Book Publishing: The Effects of Digital Innovation on the Industry*. New York: Palgrave Macmillan, 2016.
DOI: 10.1057/9781137576217.0009.

In Chapter 3, we indicated that there is a downward trend for employment in the publishing industry. This fact is mirrored by the increasing unemployment rate, as indicated in Table 4A.1 in the appendix to this chapter. The unemployment rate moved from 3.0 percent in 2000 to 4.4 percent in 2008, jumping as high as 5.0 percent in the interim years of 2003 and 2004. However, those rates are not above normal relative to the rest of the economy, indicating that the publishing industry has a stable influence on the national unemployment rate.

The book industry relies on a variety of labor processes. Exploring the health and prospects of the industry in the 1990s, a study found that "a thousand dollars of investment must be tied up for every thousand dollars of publisher's annual revenue" (Dennis, LaMay, and Pease, 1997, p. 5). Much of that expense is the cost of labor: editors, designers, production staff, and sales force. But capital advances have to be procured as well to pay these workers before the book is published. This means that both labor and capital, alongside technology, are important inputs for the production process. Indeed, some would say the industry is capital intensive.

Productivity

We now investigate productivity in the publishing industry. Traditionally, productivity is defined with respect to the factors of production, such as labor and capital. Using only labor input would be an indicator of labor productivity, *ceteris paribus*, if variations with respect to capital per worker, changes in technology, scale of output, and capacity utilization remain constant (Alterman and Jacobs, 1961, p. 281).

Table 4A.4 indicates the annual percent change in the industry's productivity since 1988 based on census computation. Annual productivity has been less than 1 percent—well below average annual changes in compensation for the period. Table 3A.5 displays the indices behind the data, which we used to analyze the contribution of wages to productivity.

According to Arrow, Chenery, Minhas, and Solow (1961), variation in wages explains over 85 percent of the variation in productivity in over 20 industries. In the Printing and Publishing industry, the authors found the variation to be 0.867 at the 95 percent confidence level (Arrow, 1985, 5:55–56). They drew implications for the type of relevant production function based on those high response rates of productivity to wages, laying the precedence for Constant Elasticity of Substitution (CES) over a Cobb-Douglas type of production function for the prediction of output, factor prices, rentals on capital, and wages (ibid., p. 237).

Following the Arrow et al. logarithmetic specification (Arrow et al., 1985, p. 55) hypothesis, we have fitted the data of Table 4A.5 to various equations relating productivity to labor cost. The results of Table 4.1 for these regressions suggest that wages account for 17–22 percent of the variation in productivity. This is about two-third less than the 0.867 estimates propounded by Arrow et al. for the printing and publishing industry, suggesting that we should not ignore other factors besides wage for variation in productivity.

Production function for book publishing

Traditional production function fits the equation of output on inputs. For the book industry, the selection of these variables is not straightforward. Our analysis uses wage and salary workers for labor inputs and data on the output of the book industry by R.R. Bowker. Capital is hard to come by. The literature suggests that we may take the sum of cash, notes, and accounts receivable, inventory, and depreciable assets as a measure of capital for the retail industry (Schwartzman, 1971, p. 65). Databases do not carry symmetric coverage of companies for the industry. We have sampled several definitions of capital data from the S&P Compustat Tapes and Mergent data bases for the NAICS 51130

TABLE 4.1 *Productivity explained by wages, 1989–2007 BLS data*

	Output/workers	Output/worker	Output/hour	Output/hour
Constant	3.64	3.80	3.79	3.90
	(12.11)***	(11.68)***	(20.02)***	(19.67)***
Unit lab. cost	0.22		0.17	
	(3.29)***		(4.20)***	
Labor compen.		0.18		0.15
		(2.56)***		(3.49)***
R^2	0.67	63	0.61	0.56
D. W.	2.05	1.94	2.04	1.96

Note: *** indicates 99 level of significance. AR(1) corrections were made for auto correlation. Data is from Table 4A.5.

definition of the book publishing industry in order to get a production function that is the best fit.

The specification of the production function is also a matter of concern. We have vied for the one that makes the Cobb-Douglas type function yield constant returns for capital and labor. Traditionally, the unrestricted form of the function can be restricted to have the labor and capital coefficients reach unity. In the logarithmic form, the Cobb-Douglas function with coefficients α for labor, and β for capital, where Q is book output, L is labor, K is capital, u is a random error term, and ln is the natural log as in Eq.4.1:

$$\ln(Q) = \ln(A) + \alpha \ln(L) + \beta(K) + u. \qquad (Eq\ 4.1)$$

The production function allows us to investigate several aspects of the book publishing industry, which strives to gain economies of scale from the production, distribution, and consumption sides of its operations. We wish to examine all of these angles.

Production economies

On the production side, we wish to ascertain whether the industry is operating under constant returns to scale (CRS), increasing returns (IRS), or decreasing returns (DRS). Because the very nature of the production process has changed due to innovation, it is almost intuitive that economies of scales were increasing. But we need to arrive at that understanding from an analysis of the data, with some hypothesis such as the following:

> **Hypothesis: (CRS, IRS, or DRS): (Production Run):** Economies of scale were dominant in publishers' batch runs, which technology has now changed.

In the traditional book industry, the high cost of typesetting was spread over the number of runs—absent in small batches and present in large batches. As far back as 1992, Joseph Dionne, chairman and CEO of McGraw-Hill, wrote that with the advent of digital technology "a 2,000-book run can be followed by a 50-book run, which can then be followed by 450-book run, without stopping" (Dennis, LaMay, and Pease, 1997, p. 25). By 2000, the technology was well advanced, and the marginal cost of producing an additional book was pushed to zero (Ronte, 2001, p. 18).

Table 4.2 examines the ratio of Average Costs to Marginal Cost (AC(q)/MC(q)) hypothesis for recent years for which data is available. We note that AC(q) was consistently falling for operating, personnel, material, and service costs, while MC(q) identifies that the Stage I phase of production is associated with increasing marginal returns. Decreases for the total of operating costs and the personnel and services components are in accord with this phase I.

What to make of the negative of material and other costs? We have noted the argument that MC = 0 for this industry, implying that once sunk cost has occurred, it no longer matters to the decision process of whether to produce a small or large production run. That MC is negative (TC falling) can be ascribed to either incorrect data, or some costs being ignored. Assuming the latter, we know that technological progress has greatly changed the way books are produced, distributed, and consumed. The industry has been gaining positive externality from new technology, and for its profit maximization to make sense with negative MC, we need to incorporate this idea into its profit maximization. This can be expressed via an equation:

Maximize $pq - c(qx) - u(q,z)$, so that $c'(q) = p - u'(q,z)$, where p is price, c is costs, z is the externality variable. Since z captures the spillover of technology to this industry, it has the potential to make cost negative.

So far, with the falling MC, we have an idea that economies of scale are present, but the question to be explored is whether the economies are increasing or of a constant nature. We can shed further light on this matter by fitting a production function, with the restriction that the coefficients for capital and labor add to unity. Applying the restriction $\alpha + \beta = 1$, which implies that $\alpha = 1 - \beta$, allows us to fit the restricted form specification, Eq. 4.2, for constant returns to scale is:

$$\ln(Q)\ln(Q) = \ln(A) + (1-\beta)\ln(L) + \beta\ln(K) + u.$$
$$= \ln(A) + \ln(L) - \beta\ln(L) + \beta\ln(K) + u$$
$$= \ln(Q) - \ln(L) = \ln(A) + \beta[\ln(K) - \ln(l)] \quad (Eq\ 4.2)$$
$$= \ln\left(\frac{Q}{L}\right) = \ln(A) + \beta\ln\left(\frac{K}{L}\right) + u$$

Table 4.3 shows the results of fitting Eq. 2 to the various definitions of the variables. Two measures of output are investigated: book output as measured by R.R. Bowker data, and quantity sold as reported by the Book Industry Study Group. Also, two measures of capital are used: the sum of

TABLE 4.2 *Industry total scale economy, 2004–2006*

	Operating cost		Marginal	Average	Estimate
	OUT Bowker(m)	TC($m)	Cost	Cost	Scale economies
2004	0.195	15,999		82,046.15	
2005	0.2825	16,754	8,628.571	59,306.19	6.8732
2006	0.27442	16,268	6,0148.51	59,281.39	0.9856
2004–2006			3,387.06	59,281.39	17.50
Personnel cost					
2004	0.195	6,581		33,748.72	
2005	0.2825	6,634	605.7143	23,483.19	38.7694
2006	0.27442	6,703	−8,539.6	24,426.06	−2.8603
2004–2006			1,536.14	24,426.06	15.90
Material cost					
2004	0.195	560		2,871.795	
2005	0.2825	487	−834.286	1,723.894	−2.0663
2006	0.27442	465	2,722.772	1,694.483	0.6223
2004–2006			−1,196.17	1,694.48	−1.42
Services cost					
2004	0.195	3,019		15,482.05	
2005	0.2825	3,244	2,571.429	11,483.19	4.4657
2006	0.27442	3,353	−13,490.1	12,218.5	−0.9057
2007					
2004–2006			4,205.49	12,218.50	2.91
Other costs					
2004	0.195	5,839		29,943.59	
2005	0.2,825	6,389	6,285.714	22,615.93	3.5980
2006	0.27,442	5,748	79,331.68	20,946	0.2640
2007					
2004–2006			−1,145.81	20,946.00	−18.28

Source: Quantity Data: R.R. Bowker; Cost Data: Statistical Abstract of the United States (2009).

cash, notes and account receivable, inventory, and depreciable assets for the NAICS 51113 as reported by Compustat Tapes, and the Physical Plant and Equipment for that NAICS code as reported by Mergent. The results of the table correspond to the following four specifications.

EQ. 1 Output(Bowker)/Employment(BLS) = f(PPE(Mergent)/Emp, Consumer Expenditures)

EQ. 2 Output(Bowker/Employment(BLS) = f(Assets(Compustat)/Emp, Consumer Expenditures)

EQ. 3 Quantity(Compustat)/Employment(BLS) = f(PPE(Mergent)/Emp, Consumer Expenditures)

EQ. 4 Quantity(Compustat)/Employment(BLS) = f(Assets(Compustat)/Emp, Consumer Expenditures

Regarding the significance of statistics, the results of Table 4.3 show that both sources of quantity data give strong statistical results for PPE when Mergent data is used as capital, than Assets when Compustat data is used as capital. The only difference is that the BISG data did not return a significant t-value for Assets. The quantity data from both R.R. Bowker and BISG are serially correlated, indicating that production in the recent past (one or two years) is probably still counted in the current numbers, even though R.R. Bowker Company has tried to avoid backlist titles from its data.

Because we have restricted the coefficient of capital and labor to be unity, the estimated coefficient for capital is 0.79 when PPE is used and is 0.42 when Asset is used for capital. The labor coefficients will therefore be 0.21 (1−.79) and 0.58 (1−.42), respectively. The overall results of Table 4.3 give significance to the idea that the capital and labor coefficients add to unity, implying production under constant returns to scale.

TABLE 4.3 Production function, book publishing industry sample, 1998–2007

Dependent	EQ. 1 Output (Bowker)	EQ. 2 Output (Bowker)	EQ. 3 Quantity sold (BISG)	EQ. 4 Quantity sold (BISG)
Constant	8.51 (8.37)***	7.79 (12.63)***	8.19 (95.00)***	11.59 (10.11)***
PPE/Emp.	0.79 (2.85)***		0.42 (2.78)**	
Assets/Emp.		0.42 (2.48)***		0.04 (0.47)
Consumption	1.39 (7.91)***	2.0 (11.17)***	0.59 (5.95)***	0.54 (5.93)
R^2	0.95	0.94	0.91	0.81
D.W.	2.74	2.49	2.65	1.51
Adjustments	None	None	AR(1)	None

Note: The significant levels are: * = 90 percent level, ** = 95 percent level, and *** = 99 percent level.

One can validate the constant returns to scale result by yet another empirical test. According to standard econometric procedures, we can fit the production in restricted and unrestricted form, and do an F-test for the differences. However, we were able to find the following fit to make a textbook kind of F-test for our data (Studenmund, 1997, p. 253).

Unrestricted equation:

$$Log(QNBISG - B) = 2.09(3.82)^{***} + 3.1(3.72)^{***}$$
$$Log(Empall - B) + 0.69(3.34)^{***}$$
$$Log(MergentAssets - B) + AR(2) correction.$$
$$R^2 = 0.79; D.W. = 1.5\{\ \}$$

Restricted equation:

$$Log(QNBISG / MergentAsset) = 10.02(5.36)^{***} + 0.95(6.55)^{***}$$
$$Log(Empall / MergentAsset)$$
$$+ AR(1) correction.$$
$$R^2 = 0.69; D.W. = 1.6$$

Using the residual sum of squares of those equations, we fitted the following F-test. Since the test value is less than the critical value at the 99 percent confidence level, we cannot reject the null hypothesis that constant returns to scale characterize the book publishing industry for the sample period.

$$F = \frac{(0.037143 - .02991)/1}{0.02991/4} = 0.967002 < F_{1,4} = 21.2$$

Implication of returns to scale findings

The empirical finding of constant returns spotlights some controversy regarding the current market structure of the book industry. One side of the story it tells is that firms have expanded down their long-run average cost curve to exhaust economies of scale. The other side of the story is that we have witnessed firms building bookstores of inefficient size (Amazon.com excepted). The existence of these two contrary views is reconciled only if we accept a monopolistic competition market structure for the book industry.

An alternative to a monopolistic competition characterization of the book industry is to fall back on a classical view. Alfred Marshall, for instance, has argued for a "representative firm," which is an average size firm that is not struggling and has had a fairly long life with fair success and normal ability (Marshall, 1982, pp. 264–265). Barnes & Noble and Books-a-Million appear to be good examples of such representative firms. On the contrary, following Joseph Stiglitz's interpretation of Chamberlin, we may want to classify these firms as bilateral monopolists (Stiglitz, 2009, p. 63).

One empirical way to get around the theoretical concept of constant returns, and therefore avoid the problem of classifying the market structure, is to fit the unrestricted equation above. We can find restricted equations of the CES or Translog specification forms to fit the F-test, which allows us to get around the unitary elasticity of substitution between capital and labor in a Cobb-Douglas production function. Essentially, the CES function is by nature nonlinear, and cannot be transformed into a linear model (Wallis, 1973, pp. 52–62). The following CES function we examine is presented by Arrow et al. (1985, p. 62):

$$V = \gamma \left[\delta K^{-\rho} + (1-\delta) L^{-\rho} \right]^{-1/\rho} \quad \text{..................CES Model.}$$

One important characteristic of the CES model is that for $\rho = 0$, the elasticity of substitution is unity, which yields the Cobb-Douglas model. If the value of ρ lies in the interval $[-1, 0]$, then the elasticity of substitution would be greater than unity. Using the GAMS software, with CANOP nonlinear solver, we estimated a value of $\rho = 0.518$ (n = 12) for V = QNBISG L = employment, and K = Compustat-Asset. Using the same equation, but a Mergent-Asset, yields only a slight variation, $\rho = 0.501$ (n = 10). The results indicate that the substitution parameter is not unity, but greater than unity, which suggests that we should not rely on the Cobb-Douglas specification alone.

Table 4.4 illustrates the difference of findings of the translog (unrestricted) versus Cobb-Douglas (restricted) model. We follow the literature and make translog approximation of the CES (Greene, 1997, p. 695). The relations are estimated using BISG quantity data against capital defined from the Compustat data. The Bowker output and Mergent capital data do not yield significant results in translog form, and are therefore omitted. The results yield the following F-statistics.

$$F = \frac{(0.040056 - 0.021007)/1}{0.021007/4} = 3.627172 < F_{1,4} = 21.2$$

The F-test for the translog retrogression for the results in Table 4.4 does not invalidate the Cobb-Douglas specification. This result is consistent with the findings of Table 4.1, that wages alone do not explain much of the productivity in the book publishing industry. In fact, as we proceed to interpret the results of Table 4.4, we find that the results are consistent with modern concepts of increasing returns.

Let us follow a traditional way of interpreting the implied results of returns to scale. The returns-to-scale parameter for EQTL1 is $v = 64.96 - 62.02 = 2.64$, indicating increasing returns to scale because it is greater than unity. The substitution parameter between labor and capital is $\rho = (-2*2.55* (v = 2.94) / (64.96* - 62.02) = .003722)$, which is less than unity. The distribution parameter is $\delta = -62.02 / (v = 2.94) = -21.09$ The capital coefficient is

$$\frac{\partial Q}{\partial K} = -62.02 \log K + 2.55 + -1*\rho = .004 * v = 2.94 * \delta$$
$$= -21.09 * (1 + 21.09) = 3.58$$

In this chapter, we visited the production side of the book industry. The empirical analysis strives to reconcile contrary views about increasing

TABLE 4.4 *Translog approximation of CES production function, BISG quantity, and compustat capital data*

	EQ. TL0 Quantity (BISG)	EQ. TL1 Quantity (BISG)
Constant	13.86	406.29
	(2.35)***	(5.97)***
Log L	1.45	64.96
	(2.28)***	(5.92)***
Log K	0.13	−62.02
	(1.54)	(5.90)***
[Log K−LogL]²		2.55
		(5.89)***
SSR	0.040056	0.021007
D.W.	2.20	2.09
R²; Adj. R²	0.76; 0.65	0.82, 0.64

Note: The level of significance is: *** = percent level.

and constant returns to scale, using generally available data and standard econometric techniques. We embrace both the simple Cobb-Douglas and CES models of production. The former indicates constant returns with weak statistical results. The CES model indicates increasing returns. The overall view one gets is subject to wide interpretation, which underscores a monopolistic structure, or a bilateral monopolistic model. The results are also included in the modern discussion of increasing returns, which is normally attributed to the influence of modern technological advances.

Appendix

TABLE 4A.1 Unemployment rate, nonagricultural private wage, and salary workers, publishing except Internet: 2000–current

Year	January	February	March	April	May	June	July	August	September	October	November	December	Annual
2000	1.9	2.7	5.4	3	4.7	2.9	2.7	1.5	3.6	2.3	2.3	2.6	3
2001	2	2.2	3.2	3	1.2	1.8	5	4	4.3	2.5	3.3	5.6	3.1
2002	2.9	5	5.5	4.1	4.9	3	3.6	3.4	3	4.9	4.7	5.1	4.2
2003	3.5	4.6	5.1	5.4	5.4	4.1	2.9	3.9	6.6	3.1	7.1	5	4.7
2004	5.7	4.9	3.4	1.9	5	5.3	3.7	5	5.6	4.5	5.7	4.7	4.6
2005	4	3.9	4.4	4.6	5.8	4.4	5.8	3.7	4.8	3.5	3.2	2.2	4.2
2006	3	2.7	3.4	3.6	5.3	3.5	3	3.5	3.6	3	2.8	1.7	3.2
2007	4.7	5.3	3.6	2.2	4.6	2.9	2.9	3.2	1.2	1.6	2	2.9	3.2
2008	5.2	5.9	3.9	4.5	4.6	3.2	4.3	2.9	4.6	2.7	4.4	6.3	4.4
2009	7.8	5.5	7.4	10.3	12.8								

TABLE 4A.2 Book publishers: NAICS 51113, average hourly earnings of production workers

Year	January	February	March	April	May	June	July	August	September	October	November	December	Annual
2003	15.29	15.63	15.29	15.31	15.61	16.07	16.17	16.06	15.8	15.9	15.54	15.72	15.7
2004	16.12	16.1	16.23	16.22	16.34	16.5	16.64	16.66	16.77	16.55	16.77	16.59	16.47
2005	16.66	16.55	16.64	16.9	17.05	16.69	17.05	17.13	17.32	17.56	17.54	17.72	17.07
2006	17.86	18.21	18.55	18.62	18.34	18.42	18.74	18.89	19.13	19.33	18.81	18.98	18.66
2007	19.28	19.46	19.18	19.54	19.51	19.12	19.41	19.88	20.14	20.02	19.98	20.12	19.63
2008	19.84	19.79	20.45	20.64	20.82	20.85	21.05	21.02	21.71	21.7	21.46	21.64	20.93
2009	21.2	21.21	21.17	21.33									

TABLE 4A.3 Industry technical data

Obs Year	CompuStat Assets Measure ($b)	Mergent PPE Measure ($m)	Payroll Cost ($b)	Material Cost ($b)	Operating Expense ($b)
1985					
1986				3.1	
1987				3.663	
1988					
1989	NA	NA	2.132000	4.366	
1990	NA	NA	2.300000	4.466	
1991	NA	NA	2.514000	5.001	
1992	NA	NA	2.676000	5.338	
1993	NA	NA	2.700000		
1994	NA	NA	2.936000	5.827	
1995	15027.36	NA	3.022000	6.303	
1996	15426.51	NA	3.128000	6.601	
1997	14847.13	NA	3.643000		
1998	21100.50	NA	3.781000		
1999	20096.00	1128.030	3.767000		
2000	21672.60	1191.710	4.310000		
2001	18445.69	1088.160	4.803000		
2002	21156.97	1155.120	4.880000		
2003	23035.05	1375.920	4.257000		
2004	23912.07	1440.870	6.581000	0.56	16.415
2005	23907.36	1455.180	6.634000	0.487	17.375
2006	10405.92	1177.280	6.703000	0.465	
2007	NA	1304.570	NA		
2008	NA	1241.130	NA		

TABLE 4A.4 NAICS 511130, book publishers. Annual percentage change of industry productivity data, 1988–current

Year	Labor productivity (%)	Output per worker (%)	Output (%)	workers Hours (%)	All workers (%)	Unit labor cost (%)	Labor compensation (%)
1988	−2.8	−2.6	3.6	6.5	6.4	7	10.8
1989	−3.8	−2.4	−2.2	1.6	0.2	9.5	7.1
1990	1.7	2.4	2.9	1.1	0.4	5.6	8.6
1991	7.8	7.6	4.7	−2.9	−2.7	5	9.9
1992	−1.8	−2.1	−4.2	−2.4	−2.1	9.6	5.1
1993	3.7	4.7	6.7	2.9	1.9	−0.4	6.3
1994	−1.5	0.3	2.3	3.8	2	0.9	3.2
1995	−1.4	−1.8	−0.3	1	1.5	5.3	4.9
1996	0.1	−2.9	−1.3	−1.4	1.6	3.2	1.9
1997	5.9	4.6	6.6	0.6	1.9	10.2	17.5
1998	−8.5	−8.7	−9.2	−0.8	−0.6	13.1	2.7
1999	10.1	12.8	9.8	−0.3	−2.7	−4.9	4.4
2000	3.1	4.4	3.9	0.8	−0.5	0.1	4
2001	0.3	1.4	1.1	0.8	−0.3	2.1	3.2
2002	2.1	1.9	−1.6	−3.6	−3.5	1.8	0.1
2003	−3.1	0.4	−7.8	−4.8	−8.2	9.5	1
2004	−5	−0.7	4.5	10	5.3	0.3	4.8
2005	0.1	−4.3	−4	−4.1	0.3	13.4	8.9
2005	1.8	−3.2	−3.6	−5.3	−0.3	7.4	3.5
2007	6.1	4.7	2.2	−3.7	−2.4	0.6	2.8
Average	0.745	0.825	0.705	−0.01	−0.09	4.965	5.535

Source: BLS Data: ftp://ftp.bls.gov/pub/special.requests/opt/dipts/ipr.airt.txt.

TABLE 4A.5 Productivity, costs, and output indices, 1987–current (1997 = 100) BLS data

Year	Lab. index: Total labor hours	Labor productivity: output per hours	Output per worker	Labor compen. index	Unit labor cost index	Output index
1987	90.036	92.865	93.216	48.754	58.309	83.613
1988	95.923	90.295	90.77	54.041	62.393	86.614
1989	97.493	86.864	88.557	57.852	68.313	84.686
1990	98.58	88.37	90.702	62.856	72.153	87.115
1991	95.672	95.29	97.562	69.091	75.786	91.166
1992	93.333	93.603	95.511	72.591	83.092	87.362
1993	96.019	97.081	99.978	77.151	82.766	93.216
1994	99.71	95.666	100.293	79.638	83.488	95.388
1995	100.752	94.362	98.453	83.571	87.903	95.072
1996	99.366	94.437	95.629	85.131	90.722	93.838
1997	100	100	100	100	100	100
1998	99.234	91.472	91.341	102.696	113.137	90.771
1999	98.953	100.696	103.073	107.183	107.569	99.641
2000	99.731	103.781	107.647	111.456	107.684	103.502
2001	100.495	104.076	109.133	115.028	109.979	104.591
2002	96.849	106.213	111.198	115.149	111.94	102.867
2003	92.233	102.869	111.686	116.249	122.523	94.879
2004	101.444	97.749	110.863	121.873	122.905	99.161
2005	97.289	97.849	106.068	132.665	139.359	95.197
2006	92.17	99.615	102.65	137.374	149.62	91.815
2007	88.755	105.692	107.453	141.169	150.488	93.807

TABLE 4A.6 Regression results for productivity on wages

System: SYSARROW
Estimation Method: Seemingly Unrelated Regression (Marquardt)
Date: 08/07/09 Time: 13:08
Sample: 1990 2007
Included observations: 19
Total system (balanced) observations 18
Iterate coefficients after one-step weighting matrix
Convergence achieved after: 1 weight matrix, 5 total coef iterations

	Coefficient	Std. error	t-statistic	Prob.
C(1)	3.794251	0.189510	20.02139	0.0000
C(2)	0.174293	0.041509	4.198967	0.0008
C(3)	0.191169	0.223309	0.856074	0.4054
Determinant residual covariance		0.000976		

Equation: LOG(BLSOUTPERHR) = C(1) + C(2)*LOG(BLSUNITLABCOST) + [AR(1) = C(3)]

Observations: 18

R-squared	0.606265	Mean dependent var	4.586460
Adjusted R-squared	0.553767	S.D. dependent var	0.051243
S.E. of regression	0.034230	Sum squared resid	0.017576
Durbin-Watson stat	2.037400		

System: SYSARROW
Estimation Method: Seemingly Unrelated Regression (Marquardt)
Date: 08/07/09 Time: 13:05
Sample: 1990 2007
Included observations: 19
Total system (balanced) observations 18
Iterate coefficients after one-step weighting matrix
Convergence achieved after: 1 weight matrix, 5 total coef iterations

	Coefficient	Std. error	t-statistic	Prob.
C(1)	3.899371	0.198191	19.67485	0.0000
C(2)	0.149803	0.042938	3.488818	0.0033
C(3)	0.238650	0.222731	1.071470	0.3009
Determinant residual covariance		0.001092		

Equation: LOG(BLSOUTPERHR) = C(1) + C(2)*LOG(BLSLABCOMP) + [AR(1) = C(3)]

Observations: 18

R-squared	0.559819	Mean dependent var	4.586460
Adjusted R-squared	0.501128	S.D. dependent var	0.051243
S.E. of regression	0.036193	Sum squared resid	0.019649
Durbin-Watson stat	1.961823		

System: SYSARROW
Estimation Method: Seemingly Unrelated Regression (Marquardt)
Date: 08/07/09 Time: 13:03
Sample: 1990 2007
Included observations: 19
Total system (balanced) observations 18
Iterate coefficients after one-step weighting matrix
Convergence achieved after: 1 weight matrix, 5 total coef iterations

	Coefficient	Std. error	t-statistic	Prob.
C(1)	3.800767	0.325296	11.68402	0.0000
C(2)	0.179672	0.070087	2.563543	0.0216
C(3)	0.440662	0.206990	2.128901	0.0502

Determinant residual covariance 0.001490

Equation: LOG(BLSOUTPERWORKER) = C(1) + C(2)*LOG(BLSLABCOMP) + [AR(1) = C(3)]
Observations: 18

R-squared	0.633942	Mean dependent var	4.624711
Adjusted R-squared	0.585134	S.D. dependent var	0.065639
S.E. of regression	0.042278	Sum squared resid	0.026811
Durbin-Watson stat	1.937367		

System: SYSARROW
Estimation Method: Seemingly Unrelated Regression (Marquardt)
Date: 08/07/09 Time: 12:13
Sample: 1990 2007
Included observations: 19
Total system (balanced) observations 18
Iterate coefficients after one-step weighting matrix
Convergence achieved after: 1 weight matrix, 5 total coef iterations

	Coefficient	Std. error	t-statistic	Prob.
C(1)	3.644317	0.300975	12.10839	0.0000
C(2)	0.215583	0.065612	3.285704	0.0050
C(3)	0.405024	0.214964	1.884149	0.0791

Determinant residual covariance 0.001331

Equation: LOG(BLSOUTPERWORKER) = C(1) + C(2)*LOG(BLSUNITLABCOST) + [AR(1) = C(3)]
Observations: 18

R-squared	0.672890	Mean dependent var	4.624711
Adjusted R-squared	0.629275	S.D. dependent var	0.065639
S.E. of regression	0.039965	Sum squared resid	0.023959
Durbin-Watson stat	2.045517		

Production Aspects: Employment, Manpower, and Productivity   89

Dependent Variable: LOG(QNBISG/(EMPALL/1000000))
Method: Least Squares
Date: 07/23/09 Time: 11:00
Sample(adjusted): 1995 2006
Included observations: 12 after adjusting endpoints

Variable	Coefficient	Std. Error	t-Statistic	Prob.
C	11.59428	1.146733	10.11071	0.0000
LOG((COMPUSTATASS/ 1000)/((EMPALL/1000000)))	0.040224	0.086017	0.467629	0.6512
LOG(CONEX PEN/1000)	0.537035	0.090627	5.925780	0.0002
R-squared	0.805162	Mean dependent var		10.28427
Adjusted R-squared	0.761865	S.D. dependent var		0.152592
S.E. of regression	0.074464	Akaike info criterion		−2.144695
Sum squared resid	0.049903	Schwarz criterion		−2.023469
Log likelihood	15.86817	F-statistic		18.59614
Durbin-Watson stat	1.515004	Prob(F-statistic)		0.000636

TABLE 4A.7   *(Additional data) Regression results for productivity on wages*

Dependent Variable: LOG(QNBISG/(EMPALL/1000000))
Method: Least Squares
Date: 07/23/09 Time: 10:52
Sample(adjusted): 2000 2007
Included observations: 8 after adjusting endpoints
Convergence achieved after 9 iterations

Variable	Coefficient	Std. error	t-statistic	Prob.
C	8.190067	1.607976	5.093400	0.0070
LOG((PPEMERGENT/1000)/ ((EMPALL/1000000)))	0.418452	0.150715	2.776438	0.0500
LOG(CONEXPEN/1000)	0.579946	0.097551	5.945070	0.0040
AR(1)	−0.334002	0.314677	−1.061413	0.3483
R-squared	0.912594	Mean dependent var		10.38782
Adjusted R-squared	0.847040	S.D. dependent var		0.153585
S.E. of regression	0.060067	Akaike info criterion		−2.479847
Sum squared resid	0.014432	Schwarz criterion		−2.440126
Log likelihood	13.91939	F-statistic		13.92117
Durbin-Watson stat	2.653025	Prob(F-statistic)		0.013900

Dependent Variable: LOG(OUTBOWKER/EMPALL)
Method: Least Squares
Date: 07/23/09 Time: 10:34
Sample(adjusted): 1995 2006
Included observations: 12 after adjusting endpoints

Variable	Coefficient	Std. error	t-statistic	Prob.
C	7.791554	0.616829	12.63162	0.0000
LOG((COMPUSTATASS/1000)/ (EMPALL))	0.421684	0.169927	2.481559	0.0349
LOG(CONEXPEN/1000)	1.999563	0.179033	11.16867	0.0000
R-squared	0.941006	Mean dependent var		0.430728
Adjusted R-squared	0.927896	S.D. dependent var		0.547823
S.E. of regression	0.147103	Akaike info criterion		−0.783055
Sum squared resid	0.194753	Schwarz criterion		−0.661828
Log likelihood	7.698330	F-statistic		71.77846
Durbin-Watson stat	2.493744	Prob(F-statistic)		0.000003

Dependent Variable: LOG(OUTBOWKER/EMPALL)
Method: Least Squares
Date: 07/23/09 Time: 10:13
Sample(adjusted): 1999 2007
Included observations: 9 after adjusting endpoints

Variable	Coefficient	Std. error	t-statistic	Prob.
C	8.505991	1.016823	8.365263	0.0002
LOG((PPEMERGENT/1000)/ (EMPALL))	0.784916	0.275668	2.847322	0.0293
LOG(CONEXPEN/1000)	1.386393	0.175379	7.905124	0.0002
R-squared	0.952329	Mean dependent var		0.784838
Adjusted R-squared	0.936438	S.D. dependent var		0.379821
S.E. of regression	0.095758	Akaike info criterion		−1.592774
Sum squared resid	0.055018	Schwarz criterion		−1.527033
Log likelihood	10.16748	F-statistic		59.93084
Durbin-Watson stat	2.735501	Prob(F-statistic)		0.000108

TABLE 4A.8 Results use for translog/CES model of table T2-4 system: SYSKAMENTA1

Estimation Method: Seemingly Unrelated Regression (Marquardt)
Date: 08/06/09   Time: 12:08
Sample: 1998 2006
Included observations: 12
Total system (balanced) observations 9
Iterate coefficients after one-step weighting matrix
Convergence achieved after: 1 weight matrix, 7 total coef iterations

	Coefficient	Std. error	t-statistic	Prob.
C(1)	406.2870	68.08163	5.967645	0.0040
C(2)	−62.02375	10.51220	−5.900171	0.0041
C(3)	64.95885	10.95883	5.927534	0.0041
C(4)	2.544328	0.432138	5.887761	0.0042
C(7)	0.539888	0.280654	1.923682	0.1267
Determinant residual covariance	0.002334			

Equation: LOG(QNBISG) = C(1) + C(2)*LOG(COMPUSTATASS/1000) + C(3)*LOG(EMPALL/1000000) + C(4)*(LOG(COMPUSTATASS/1000) − LOG(EMPALL/1000000))^2 + [AR(3) = C(7)]
Observations: 9

R-squared	0.820683	Mean dependent var	0.956263
Adjusted R-squared	0.641365	S.D. dependent var	0.121011
S.E. of regression	0.072469	Sum squared resid	0.021007
Durbin-Watson stat	2.095437		

System: SYS1
Estimation Method: Seemingly Unrelated Regression (Marquardt)
Date: 08/06/09   Time: 09:26
Sample: 1996 2006
Included observations: 12
Total system (balanced) observations 11
Iterate coefficients after one-step weighting matrix
Convergence achieved after: 1 weight matrix, 19 total coef iterations

	Coefficient	Std. Error	t-Statistic	Prob.
C(1)	13.85661	5.898766	2.349068	0.0512
C(2)	0.133134	0.086289	1.542879	0.1668
C(3)	1.448813	0.636072	2.277749	0.0568
C(4)	1.192415	0.215285	5.538763	0.0009
Determinant residual covariance	0.003641			

Equation: LOG(QNBISG) = C(1) + C(2)*LOG(COMPUSTATASS/1000) + C(3)*LOG(EMPALL/1000000) + [AR(1) = C(4)]
Observations: 11

R-squared	0.755058	Mean dependent var	0.925705
Adjusted R-squared	0.650083	S.D. dependent var	0.127879
S.E. of regression	0.075646	Sum squared resid	0.040056
Durbin-Watson stat	2.197130		

TABLE 4A.9 GAMS model for the extraction of substitution parameters
$title estimate of CES parameters
set i 'observations' /i1*i12/;
set j 'parameters' /L,K,VA/;
table data(i,j)

	L	K	VA
i1	8.57e-05	15.027362	2.186
i2	8.76e-05	15.426511	2.219
i3	8.92e-05	14.847126	2.18
i4	8.86e-05	21.1005	2.402
i5	8.72e-05	20.095996	2.505
i6	8.83e-05	21.6726	2.461
i7	8.75e-05	18.445689	2.358
i8	8.34e-05	21.156966	2.365
i9	7.88e-05	23.03505	2.339
i10	8.18e-05	23.91207	2.966
i11	8.24e-05	23.907362	3.078
i12	8.26e-05	10.405922	3.1

;

Parameters
L(i) 'Travail'
K(i) 'Capital'
VA(i) 'valeur ajoutee'
;
L(i) = data(i,'L');
K(i) = data(i,'K');
VA(i) = data(i,'VA');
Variables
gamma 'log du parametre d efficience'
delta 'parametre de distribution'
zeta 'parametre de distribution'
rho 'parametre de substitution'
sigma 'elasticite de substition'
* eta 'homogeneity parameter'
residual(i) 'terme error'
sse 'somme des erreurs au carre'
;
Equations
Fit(i) 'model nonlinear'
obj 'objective'
;
obj...sse = e = sum(i,sqr(residual(i)));
fit(i)...log(VA(i)) = e =
gamma − (1/rho)*log[delta*L(i)**(-rho) + (zeta)*K(i)**(-rho)]
+ residual(i);
*initial values
rho.l = 1;

```
delta.l =.01;
*delta.up = +inf;
zeta.lo =.98;
zeta.up = +inf;
gamma.l = 1;
*eta.l = 1;
model nls /obj,fit/;
option nlp = conopt;
*option nlp = minos5;
*option nlp = pathnlp;
solve nls minimizing sse using nlp;
display gamma.l, delta.l,zeta.l,rho.l,sse.l;
sigma.L = 1/(1 + rho.L);
display sigma.L;
sigma.L = 1/(1 + rho.L);
display sigma.L;
```

Source: Adapted from unpublished source—the estimation of the elasticity of substitution of a CES production function: Case of Tunisia by Haykel Hadj Salem, *GAINS—University of Maine* [web].

5
Distribution Aspects of the Industry

Abstract: *Distribution channels for books have evolved from small bookstores, to larger superstores, to the more impersonal Internet. Larger bookstores seem to have a dominant position in these activities through mergers and cooperations, yet this does not show up as high concentration for the industry. On the average, the concentration seems to be held in check from cooperation with smaller independent firms for the purpose of reaching customers in the suburbs or as independent suppliers on the Internet. Nevertheless, sales remain responsive to concentration, which in turn is responsive to mergers and an index of market power. Some modern distribution problems are also related to inventory management.*

Ramrattan, Lall, and Michael Szenberg. *Revolutions in Book Publishing: The Effects of Digital Innovation on the Industry.* New York: Palgrave Macmillan, 2016.
DOI: 10.1057/9781137576217.0010.

> Businessmen are...constantly devising and experimenting with new arrangements which involve the use of different factors of production. (Marshall, 1982, p. 550)

Introduction

Economists are interested in the distribution aspects of the book publishing industry in order to study bigness, survival, and efficiency. Such a study sheds light on the industry's levels of concentration, pricing policies, mergers, unit cost structure, and profit.

Today books are distributed through book publishers such as McGraw-Hill, bookstore chains such as Barnes & Noble, and independent sellers. The dynamics of the Internet have made the distribution channels hard to understand. Amazon.com, Barnes and Noble, Books-a-Million, and the recently extinct Borders Group are the largest players in the book industry on the Internet. In addition, as of January 31, 2009, Barnes and Noble had 778 bookstores (Firm, 2008, 10K, p. 5), and Borders Group had 1018–515 superstores, 386 mail-base and other stores, and 117 from merging with Paper Chase (ibid., p. 1).

It is clear that the Web creates stiff competition for brick-and-mortar bookstores, assuming a stable economy. As large as the 2008 store numbers may seem, they represent a downslide of 1,008 stores for Barnes & Noble and 1,122 for Borders when compared with the numbers from 1996 (Bekken, 1997/1998, p. 9). The decline in the number of bookstores was because of increasing merger activities. From 1990 to 1995, 300 mergers occurred, but from 1996 to 2001, that number increased to 380 (Greco, 2005, p. 51). In an earlier study, Albert Greco concluded that "there is no empirical evidence, after more than thirty-five years of mergers and acquisitions, that exceptionally high or patently illegal concentration levels were evident in the consumer book industry in the United States by 1995 and 1996" (Greco, 2000, p. 334).

The advent of the Internet has substantially changed the nature of competition in book distribution. The market is now bifurcated into the more impersonal Internet, and the more personal, sociocultural superstores. Large chains can now collude with small sellers to expand their market by allowing many independent sellers access to their websites. When you buy from an authorized seller through BarnesandNoble.com, for instance, you are greeted with this statement: "We have forwarded your Used & Out of Print Book order to the Authorized Seller(s) offering the item(s) below. Used and out-of-print books are shipped directly to you by the Authorized Sellers. Each seller is responsible for confirming their acceptance of your order, and you will receive a separate email once the seller has done so." Independent buyers also gain from shopping around on websites in search of inexpensive books, thereby competing with the large discounts that chains traditionally receive from publishers.

Two distribution hypotheses

We first subject the distribution of books to two traditional industrial organization hypotheses, one by Joe S. Bain and one by George Stigler, that dominated the literature for decades. The first hypothesis is a traditional one that can be stated as follows:

> **Hypothesis 1 (BAIN):** *Concentration encourages cooperation between firms, creating potential for large profits.*

We recognize Hypothesis 1 as Joe Bain's argument (Bain, 1951, 1956). Large firms operate at a minimum efficient size (MES) and enjoy lower costs, which enhances profit. Smaller firms are sometimes denied reaching efficiency because of their inability to raise large enough capital to achieve the MES. In the book industry, however, we believe there are countertendencies to these arguments. One is that larger firms were colluding or merging with small ones to reach the suburban markets before the advent of the Internet. With the Internet, large firms are also engaging small firms on their websites. A look at the concentration ratios may spotlight the fact that the tug-of-war between large and small firms is settling over time.

Table 5.1 indicates the existence of over 3,000 firms in 2002. While the number of large publishers is few, small publishers still fill important roles, for instance, putting out products of literary quality that do not have mass market sales potential. Although the technology for producing a book may be standardized, the product is differentiated by various services offered by publishers and sellers. The size of a book run can economize on costs and therefore translate into profits, which can be captured through price-cost margins over time. One way to tie up some of these issues is with a second hypothesis.

Hypothesis 2(Stigler): *Small firms recognize and reward workers' ability more than large firms.*

George Stigler has made the great observation that "[m]en should in general enter smaller companies the greater their ability" (Stigler, 1968, p. 204). Stigler proffers the hypothesis that "small firms are more likely to absorb profits in the form of larger salaries for owner-managers," biasing the reported profits of small firms downwards (Hay and Morris, 1979, p. 207). Lolis Eric Elie called book publishing "an industry that rewards creativity, treasures personal taste, and provides opportunities to combine work with a socially responsible endeavor" (Elie, 1991). In addition to editorial work, publishing offers career potential for individuals with backgrounds in business, marketing, sales, graphic design, and computer applications. Traditionally, however, "low entry-level salaries, long hours, and slow advancement have deterred those who tried their hand in the field" (ibid.).

Table 5.1 displays census data on industry trends for various years in which the Census of Manufacturers was taken. It is surprising to find that the four (C4) and eight (C8) firms' concentration ratios are so low. Given the large number of firms, the C20 ratio shows that the larger-rank 20 firms account for over 50 percent of the value of shipment, suggesting that market power is latent in the book distribution channels.

Another source of concentration measures is the Herfindahl-Hirschman Index (HHI), which is a sum of squares of the firm's market share. The index has an upper bound of 10,000 (the square of 100 percent). The norm is that if the computed index is less than 1,000, then the industry is unconcentrated. High concentration is indicated by an index of at least 1,800, and moderate concentration by an index of 1,000–1,800.

We have computed the HHI index for firms taken from the Compustat data base. The firm's sales are taken as a percent of the total sales for the industry published by the Book Industry Sales Trends. The data is consistent for eight firms from 1989 to 1999, and sparse for the more recent years. Table 5.2 shows the index from the squares of the firms' shares.

Comparing Tables 5.1 and 5.2, it is a bit of an anomaly that the concentration ratio is approximately 40 in the more recent years. The increase is an issue because of "NAICS groups establishments that use similar production processes together. While substitutability on the production side is relevant for market definition, we should also like goods

TABLE 5.1 Distribution aspects of book publishing (number of establishments and CR ratios)

Year	Number of firms	Value of Shipment	Concentration ratios				Number of mergers	Margin all cost	Margin mat. cost	Margin pay. cost
			C4	C8	C20	C50				
1947	635	463900	18	29	48	0	0			
1954	804	665200	21	32	51	0	0			
1958	883	1000900	16	29	48	69	0			
1963	936	1534600	20	33	56	76	12			
1967	963	2060200	20	32	57	77	23			
1972	1120	2856900	19	31	56	77	8			
1977	1650	4793900	17	30	57	74	22			
1982	2007	7740000	17	30	56	75	9		0.976	0.956
1987	2182	12619500	24	38	62	78	26	3.238	0.972	0.944
1992	2504	16753100	23	38	62	77	53	3.099	0.971	0.942
1997	2541	22977000					58	3.093	0.977	0.940
2002	3242		40.7	55.2	72.7	81	84	3.117	0.967	0.900
2007										

Source: Various issues of the Economic Censuses; Census of Manufacturers. Mergers are from Greco (1997, 2005), where 2001 was used for 2002. CR for 1992, the first year of transition for NAICS, were used in 1997. Material and Payroll margins are based on the price of Hardbacks only.

TABLE 5.2 HHI calculation

Year	Harcourt General Inc.	Goodheart-Willcox Co. Inc.	Houghton Mifflin Co.	Mcgraw-Hill Companies	Nelson-Thomas Inc.	Sadlier: Wiliam H. Inc.	Scholastic Corp.	Wiley (John) & Sons	HHI index
1989	13.73	0.06	2.87	12.68	0.42	0.14	2.65	2.00	368.69
1990	14.65	0.08	2.84	13.05	0.50	0.13	2.85	1.59	403.73
1991	23.22	0.07	3.00	12.48	0.60	0.13	3.14	1.59	716.73
1992	22.93	0.07	2.78	12.56	0.84	0.12	3.38	1.67	706.37
1993	21.23	0.07	2.66	12.62	1.31	0.11	3.63	1.69	635.01
1994	17.65	0.08	2.66	15.19	1.46	0.12	4.12	1.82	571.64
1995	15.86	0.08	2.71	15.06	1.58	0.12	4.76	1.86	514.33
1996	16.56	0.08	3.56	15.26	1.21	0.13	4.80	2.14	548.97
1997	17.83	0.09	3.80	16.85	1.21	0.14	5.05	2.23	648.26
1998	19.17	0.08	3.86	16.69	1.17	0.15	5.17	2.28	694.39
1999	9.02	0.08	3.87	16.80	1.10	0.16	5.90	2.50	420.96
2000	9.80	0.10	4.18	17.42	1.21		7.98	2.50	488.25
2001		0.08	0.00	18.92	0.88		7.81	2.99	428.42
2002		0.08	4.46	17.88	0.81		7.31	3.19	403.82
2003		0.08	4.54	17.35	0.80		8.03	3.32	397.91
2004			4.45	18.20	0.82		7.21	3.38	415.04
2005			4.57	21.42	0.90		8.15	3.73	560.76
2006				22.19			7.73	4.38	571.31
2007				18.18			5.92	4.49	385.58
2008				14.67					215.21

Source: Firms' share are from Compustat Data; Shares are expressed as % of BISG sales data.

that consumers view as closely substitutable to be grouped together in a market. Because of the focus on production processes, some markets defined by the Census Bureau are too narrow and some are too broad" (Waldman and Jensen, 2007). Since 1997, the data has been reported on a NAICS (51113) basis, while the earlier data was reported on an SIC (2731) basis. In the face of this issue, the HHI index, with a score of less than 1,000 for the 1989–1999 period for four firms, will tip the analysis on the side of nonconcentration.

To model the data for some concerns pointed out in Hypotheses I and II, we have used sales instead of profits as an independent variable because of the profit bias mentioned regarding Stigler's hypothesis. The first specification, therefore, is to make Sales data from BISG dependent on concentration. The second specification we make is that the concentration ratio should be dependent on some barriers of entry variables. Stigler has pointed out that "[t]here are no large American companies that have not grown somewhat by merger" (Stigler, 1968, p. 95). In explaining concentration, we also include the price-cost margin variable because, as Stigler said, "firm size is still governed by economies of scale (height and slope of cost curves) and demand" (ibid., p. 69). The recursive system can be stated as follows:

$$\log(Sales) = a + b * \log(concentration). \qquad (Eq\ 1)$$

$$\log(concentration) = c + d * \log(mergers) + e * \log((P-c)/c). \qquad (Eq\ 2)$$

We have estimated the recursive system twice to reflect the definitions of the price-cost margin variable in Eq. 2. The first time, we used the estimate from an earlier study in which we estimated the elasticity of demand for nine book categories, from which we computed the market power based on the Lerner index. The second time, we estimated the system using a definition of price-cost margin to reflect the concerns mentioned: that small firms tend to pay their employees or themselves a high salary, which translates to a lower profit rate. The second measure of the price-cost margin is made on data gathered on the prices for hardbacks only, for the expression (Price-Payroll costs)/Price. The same cost price data is also available for material costs, which we collected as an alternative to the wage-cost hypothesis. As Table 5.1 shows, the data suffers from a small sample size.

Table 5.3 displays our estimates. All estimates are significant except for the payroll price-cost margin. The responsiveness of sales to the four firms' concentration ratio (CR4) for just the Bain hypothesis (Eq. 1, Eq. 1A, and Eq. 1B) ranges from 2.48 to 2.78, which is substantial. One implication for Bain's hypothesis is that varying the concentration can lead to a higher payoff in terms of sales revenue.

Equations 2, 2A, and 2B in Table 5.3 show significant responses to the number of mergers. The responses vary from 0.18 to 1.1, and are all significant. For Eq. 2, a measure of market power using the Lerner index and total costs indicates that the higher the market power, the greater the concentration, and the more recursiveness, the higher the sales revenue. An attempt to split the costs data into material and payroll costs is not progressive. First, data is available only to compute those margins for hardback prices. Second, the sample size is much reduced. This attempt turns out to be unsatisfactory, a test for Stigler's hypothesis that small firms recognize and reward ability better than large firms.

Upon reading the literature, one notices that skepticism still persists about the fact that significant concentration pervades the book

TABLE 5.3 *Sales on concentration, SUR system estimates, 1963–2007 (available concentration data)*

	Eq. 1	Eq. 2	Eq. 1A	Eq. 2A	EQ. 1B	EQ. 2B
	Bain	Bain-Lerner	Bain 2	Bain-material cost	Bain 3	Bain-wage cost
Constant	−5.68 (1.92)*	−22.13 (15.9)***	−5.96 (2.02)**	1.44 (4.04)***	−6.64 (2.29)***	2.45 (5.39)***
CR4	2.48 (2.59)***		2.57 (2.69)***		2.78 (2.96)***	
Mergers		1.1 (22.14)***		0.18 (2.48)***		0.23 (2.17)**
(P−C)/P (Lerner)		18.63 (17.30)***				
P-C/P (Stigler)				−40.9 (2.71)***		1.78 (0.56)
R²	0.43	0.98	0.42	0.88	0.42	0.64
Number of observations	9	4	9	5	9	5

Note: *** = 99% level; ** = 95% level; and * = 90% level of confidence.

publishing industry. In the face of the concentration and HHI analysis we have done, such skepticism can now only be grounded on whether the market definition in both the SIC and NAICs concepts is too broad. To the extent that books are divided into many categories—Adult trade, Professional, Juvenile, and so on— it is obvious that substitution chains will break down from the point of view of the consumer to create much narrower markets. Every schoolchild knows that they are unwilling to substitute a Juvenile for a Professional text. Thus, the SIC and NAICs definitions are clearly too broad, leading to an underestimation of concentration in the book industry. It is desirable to have test runs for each book category, but this is not possible with the data at hand, since the independent variable in Table 5.1 refers to all the categories and not just one.

Hypotheses 1 and 2 do not exhaust all the concerns in coping with distribution in the book publishing industry. For instance, Fritz Machlup (1962, p. 208) found this amazing fact: "The number of books published was greater in 1914 than in any year thereafter until 1953." We can list several hypotheses on the retail side of the industry as well, namely, that small stores and sellers tend to decline over time because of the increase in wages and other changes, that the number of sales per person in small stores tend to be less than in large stores, that the average earnings in small stores are less than in larger ones. We approach these additional hypotheses as part of the whole of the distribution data to which we now turn. In many ways, these hypotheses are suitable, appropriate, and traditional to explain how the distribution data unfolds.

Other distribution hypotheses

We used census data from 1992, 1997, and 2002 to examine distribution of the retail side of the book industry based on the economic census. The distribution characteristics we examined relate to the employment size of establishments, single and multiple unit firms, and the employment size of firms. We focused on how the retail book industry is structured regarding employment in firms and establishments, and the number of establishments within firms. We conducted yearly comparative analysis for three categories of booksellers: general, specialty, and college bookstores.

The data in Table 5.4 indicates that the US book industry has been contracting in size since 1992, as measured by the decline in the number of establishments: from 12,887 in 1992, to 10,860 in 2002. This decline is despite the fact that establishments with 15–19, 20–49, 50–99 and 100 plus categories were expanding. On average, the losses of establishments with fewer employees are still more than the gain in establishments with larger numbers of employees. This can best be explained by the economies of scale within the retail book industry. This makes sense due to the higher possible gross margin when a wider selection is available within the establishment. If establishments are in fact expanding their selection range, it makes sense that there would be a higher concentration of establishments with more employees.

When subcategories are observed in operated establishments, there is a slight trend of the industry to move from general bookstores to college and specialty bookstores. As Table 5.5 shows, the general store category still comprises the majority of establishments. The only subcategory that is growing in the actual number of establishments is college bookstores. The number of specialty stores declined slightly and the number of general bookstores declined to 5,526 in 2002 from 6,778 in 1997. This could be due to higher profit margins in the college market, or possibly a rise in the number of colleges, especially in the two-year, trade school, and online degree program categories.

TABLE 5.4 *Size distribution of establishments, census data: 1992, 1997, 2002*

Size of establishment	1992	1997	2002
All establishments	12,887*	12,363	10,860
Operated for the entire year	11,492	10,822	9,623
None	316	28	2
1	1,335	1,056	863
2	1,243	1,040	862
3 or 4	2,092	1,820	1,526
5 or 6	1,774	1,513	1,226
7 to 9	2,203	2,124	1,414
10–14	1,448	1,403	1,411
15–19	486	575	612
20–49	454	935	1,197
50–99	99	271	444
100 +	42	57	66

Note: *Data in the first column represents number of employees.

TABLE 5.5 Distribution of general, specialty, and college books, number of establishments by employees: 1997 versus 2002

	General			Specialty			College		
	1997	2002	Pct.	1997	2002	Pct.	1997	2002	Pct.
All establishments	7,693	6,326	−17.77	2,980	2695	−9.56	1,690	1,839	8.82
Year round	6,778	5,526	−18.47	2,529	2,402	−5.02	1,515	1,695	11.88
No employees	21	2	−90.48	7	–	–	–	–	–
1 employee	660	519	−21.36	323	281	−13.00	73	63	−13.70
2 employees	592	450	−23.99	308	258	−16.23	140	154	10.00
3 or 4 employees	988	703	−28.85	559	466	−16.64	273	357	30.77
5 or 6 employees	898	714	−20.49	406	277	−31.77	209	235	12.44
7–9 employees	1,481	822	−44.50	409	340	−16.87	234	252	7.69
10–14 employees	915	761	−16.83	285	412	44.56	203	238	17.24
15–19 employees	334	307	−8.08	119	191	60.50	122	114	−6.56
20–49 employees	654	833	27.37	104	168	61.54	177	196	10.73
50–99 employees	212	382	80.19	6	8	33.33	53	54	1.89
100 employees or more	23	33	43.48	3	1	−66.67	31	32	3.23
Not operated for the entire year	915	800	−12.57	451	293	−35.03	175	144	−17.71

While the industry is increasing establishments in the larger employee groups, the size distribution of establishments for each subcategory is still highly concentrated in the categories of fewer employees, up to and including 10–14 employees. Specialty bookstores show a higher degree of concentration of establishments, with fewer employees (up to and including the group 10–14), as compared to general and college bookstores. From 1997 to 2002 there is a definite trend for general and specialty bookstores to shift the percentage of employee groups from lower groups to higher groups. Within the college bookstores, there is very little change in the size of the establishments.

Table 5.6 shows census sales distribution data for the industry. In interpreting the data, we have adjusted for price changes based on 2002 CPI for all urban consumers. The total sales of all the establishments increased over time, although at a slower rate from 1997 to 2002 than from 1992 to 1997. At the subcategories level, college sales increased most rapidly: 12.1% from 1997 to 2002. General bookstore sales increased by 3.3%, and specialty bookstore sales increased very slightly for the same period.

Table 5.6 indicates declining sales for class size up to 15–19 employees. This loss in sales is exceeded by the gain in sales observed in the largest three class sizes, which are driving the sales growth for the

TABLE 5.6 Sales–employees distribution

	General			Specialty			College		
	1997 Sales ($)	2002 Sales ($)	Pct. Chg.	1997 Sales ($)	2002 Sales ($)	Pct. Chg.	1997 Sales ($)	2002 Sales ($)	Pct. Chg.
All establishments	8,167,174	9,482,047	16.1	1,418,656	1552806	9.5	2,789,228	4,026,131	44.3
Year round	7,892,424	9,145,143	15.9	1,337,543	1,503,022	12.4	2,706,058	3,967,672	46.6
No employees	2,799	D		2,139	–		–	–	
1 employee	71,362	D		41,293	34,851	−15.6	16,309	15,976	−2.0
2 employees	103,563	97,057	−6.3	52,282	50,370	−3.7	52,434	75,803	44.6
3 or 4 employees	277,295	224,043	−19.2	147,107	124,467	−15.4	157,899	298,016	88.7
5 or 6 employees	447,828	330,171	−26.3	176,744	112,637	−36.3	179,351	278246	55.1
7–9 employees	1,204,657	570,812	−52.6	246,338	202,239	−17.9	270,431	433,063	60.1
10–14 employees	1,029,990	731,630	−29.0	261,288	360,994	38.2	335,259	515,753	53.8
15–19 employees	545,968	434,688	−20.4	136,543	239,730	75.6	255,135	346,173	35.7
20–49 employees	2,118,213	3,224,101	52.2	226,876	339,261	49.5	611,984	952,335	55.6
50–99 employees	1,752,004	2,989,799	70.7	26,495	D		346,720	D	
100 employees	338,745	477,177	40.9	20,438	D		480,536	D	
Not operated for the entire year	274,750	336,904	22.6	81,113	49,784	−38.6	83,170	58,459	−29.7

Note: "D" indicates unreported data.

entire subcategory. This trend of sales decreasing in smaller establishments and increasing in larger establishments is almost identical in the specialty bookstores. For college bookstores, however, the trend changes. Consistent with the sales increases of college bookstores, every size establishment is growing except for those with one employee, and in turn, sales are growing in every size group except stores with one employee. One observes a positive correlation between the change in sales and size for every size group in all three subcategories. If a size category lost establishments, sales were also lost; if a size category increased, sales increased.

General discussions

The retail book industry as a whole, as measured by the number of firms, has been declining from 1992 to 2002 in a similar pattern as establishments are declining. When the size of the firm is determined by the number of employees, a decrease, or approximately no change, has been observed from 1992 to 2002 in every category with the exception of 100–249 employees and, to a lesser degree, the 1,000 employee and greater category. This leads to the conclusion that a number of large-sized firms (250 employees and larger) are having trouble growing, possibly due to large barriers to entry and tough competition.

When subcategory data is used, all three subdivisions of the book industry show a decline in the number of firms. In the college bookstores group, firms are declining, but establishments are rising. This signifies that the concentration of college book stores is rising. Fewer firms have more establishments. The concentration of the industry within the three subdivisions is constant from 1997 to 2002. There is no trend for any subgroup to get larger or smaller. In 2002, general bookstores made up 58 percent of the firm size, and also accounted for about the same percent of establishments. General bookstores have a firm establishment ratio of about 1:1.6. This suggests low concentration: many firms with few stores each. Specialty bookstores in 2002 had about the same concentration ratio, about 1.5 specialty establishments for every specialty firm. The college group, however, is only 7 percent of firms, but accounts for 18 percent of all establishments. The ratio of establishments to firms in this group is nearly 1:5. This suggests relatively high concentration: few firms with many establishments.

The distribution of employees in firms is very similar between general bookstores and specialty bookstores, with no distinct trend toward becoming more concentrated in lower-sized firms or larger-sized firms over time. The overwhelming majority of firms in these two categories are made of smaller firms, up to 19 employees. College bookstores do show a trend from 1997 to 2002 to become more concentrated in larger-sized firms. Also, college bookstores are concentrated to a lesser degree in smaller-sized firms, but small firms still make up the majority of firms.

When sales data is broken down into subcategories, analyzed by employee size of firm, and adjusted for inflation, for comparable data there is a downward trend in every size category. Sales are growing in the industry, but detailed data is not made available for larger groups, as mentioned earlier. Since all observable data for sales by the employment size of firm in each subcategory are falling, it is reasonable to assume the sales growth observed in the industry and all subcategories is coming from large firms, whose increase in sales offsets the decline in sales from smaller firms. The 1000+ category in 2002, which has only 8 firms, accounted for $10,680,403 in sales during 2002—over 70% of all sales from firms operating for the year. Large firms (250 employees and up) account for less than 0.5% of all firms, but drive all of the sales growth in the industry.

Despite the dominance in sales growth by the largest firms (defined by employees) the firms with the largest numbers of establishments are very low. Large firms (50 or more establishments) have not grown from 1992 to 2002. This could be due to the high barriers of entrance for very large firms. It is much easier for a single unit firm or a multiunit firm with few establishments to enter the market, as opposed to a very large firm with many establishments and employees. While the single unit firms clearly dominate the industry, accounting for slightly over 92 percent of all firms, both single unit and multiunit firms have been on the decline. As a percentage of the entire industry, single units are actually increasing their market share due to a declining rate that is lower than that of multiunit firms. Since 1992 single unit firms have declined by 28.36 percent, while multiunit firms have declined by just over 35 percent. Since 1992, every category of multiunit firms (up to 24 establishments) has fallen, while the larger multiunit firms have remained stable. Large multiunit firms (25 or more establishments) experienced slight growth from 1992 to 1997, but in 2002, all large multiunit firm categories contracted back to previous levels.

For all multiunit firms, sales have decreased for smaller firms and have risen dramatically in the 100 + establishment category. Multiunit firms dominate sales, with almost 83 percent of all sales in 2002, up from 69.25 in 1992. The largest-sized firms account for the overwhelming majority of sales for the entire industry; however, there were only 11 firms with over 50 establishments in 2002.

At the subcategory levels, the sales trend is similar for specialty and general bookstores as it is for total firms. Single unit firms are losing sales, while multiunit firms' sales are rising. For college bookstores, once again, the trend is different. Single unit and multiunit firms are increasing sales. When size of multiunit firms is observed, the trend is for all three subcategories to lose sales in smaller firms, leading to the conclusion that sales must be rising in the larger firms. The only noticeable exception is the 5–9 establishment category of college bookstores.

Conclusions

Traditional industrial organization spotlights many important distribution characteristics for this case study. Merger and market power do influence concentration, which in turn influences sales revenue. The distribution channels for books have evolved from bookstores, to super stores, to the Internet. Larger book stores seem to have a dominant position in these activities through mergers and corporation, yet this does not show up as high concentration for the industry. On the average for the industry, the concentration seems to be held in check from cooperation with smaller independent firms for the purpose of reaching customers in the suburbs or as independent suppliers on the Internet.

The US retail book industry as a whole has been contracting since 1992. Total firms have been declining, and the most contraction is seen in small employment categories (up to 19 employees). Mid-size firms (20–99 employees) have been stable. Large-size firms (250–999 employees) have had a slight contraction, and firms with 1,000-plus employees have seen a slight increase. Despite the trend for smaller firms to disappear, either exiting the market or becoming larger firms, small firms still make up the overwhelming majority of all firms. This is true for each of the three subcategories, general, specialty, and college firms. The subcategory concentration for firms in 2002 is: general 58 percent, specialty 35 percent, and college 7 percent. This was almost exactly the subcategory mix that existed in 1997. Sales in the subcategories have been mixed. General bookstores' sales are up 4 percent, specialty stores are down 1.5 percent, and college bookstores' sales are up about 30 percent. Almost the entire sales growth seen in the industry comes from college bookstores. Sales of specific sizes have a definite trend in subcategories; smaller and mid-size firms are losing sales and larger firms are gaining sales. This is the trend of establishments as well, with larger establishments gaining sales while smaller establishments lose sales. Establishments have a distinct trend to get larger, unlike firm size. It seems as if the college bookstores are experiencing the best results with higher sales and more establishments and firms gaining sales in smaller size organizations. Usually when a size category is contracting, sales also contract and the opposite is also true. The industry is highly concentrated in small-sized firms and establishments and single unit firms. However, the bulk of sales are concentrated within the largest firms and establishments.

6
Printing and Publishing

Abstract: *International competition requires the estimates of consumer, producer, and welfare optimum in a general equilibrium framework to account for how agents make substitution within countries. The world flow of GDP and FDI concentrates among the three regions of North America, Europe, and Asia. Our analysis proceeds with an eye for free trade according to the classical hypothesis, and a preference for domestic adjustment according to the Keynesian hypothesis for these regions. North America and Europe did much better under the classical than under the Keynesian hypothesis. Some countries, such as China and India in Asia; the United Kingdom, France, and Germany in Europe; and the United States in North America are spotlighted for more extended analysis.*

Ramrattan, Lall, and Michael Szenberg. *Revolutions in Book Publishing: The Effects of Digital Innovation on the Industry.* New York: Palgrave Macmillan, 2016.
DOI: 10.1057/9781137576217.0011.

Introduction

The international sector is broadly defined to include more than book publishing. Our aggregate data comes from Global Trade, Assistance, and Production (GTAP), which gives a broad definition of this sector under the ISIC3 two digits code 21. A more focused definition would be the four-digit ISIC 2211 sector, which is restricted to the publishing of books, brochures, musical books, and other publications. We will, however, follow two-digit classification, giving a general view of the printing and publishing industry (PPI) at the international level, because the data set at the two-digit level is more comprehensive for the world economy.

The kind of analysis we pursue requires a general equilibrium setting. In the world economy, regions compete, and varying aspects of substitution occur between the sectors as well. We can best address such aspects with models that are within the sphere of computational general equilibrium analysis (CGE), which is generally conducted across regions and sectors. The regions that have been highlighted from a modern trade perspective are the ones that account for most of the world's GDP, export and FDI flows, accentuated by the advances of the high-tech revolution. Those regions of interest have been given a name, the Triad, which refers to the three regions of North America, Europe, and Asia.

We intend to model the Triad regions for several years (1997, 2001, and 2007) for which data is available. We will therefore maintain a consistent set of countries within the Triad classification. For instance, for Europe we will examine the 25 countries in the EMU, and for North America we will use the NAFTA countries: United States, Canada, Mexico, and the rest of North America. We will make similarly consistent groupings for Asia and the Rest of the World (RoW).

In addition to a regional aggregation, we also need an aggregation for sectors. We have grouped the sectors into the printing and publishing industry, food, manufacturing, mining, textile and apparel, and all others. Again, we will maintain this grouping for the years 1997, 2001, and 2007.

Models and hypotheses

The CGE model we will investigate is of dimension 4×5, that is, four regions and five sectors. We investigate that model for varying commercial or policy perspectives. An economy can follow a liberalization or a protectionist policy, or some combination of the two. One can make two broad hypotheses about such an investigation.

> **Hypothesis 1:** [Classical]: *Free trade and output taxes are liberalizing and beneficial to all.*

In the spirit of classical economics, we intend to drop export and import tariffs by 100 percent, and also reduce taxes on output at home by that amount. The quarrel we hear in the modern media is that the world is not a level-playing field: that is, while some countries are more liberal, others are protectionist. Some have argued also that the proliferation of free trade areas, FTA, in the world should really be called preferential treatment areas, PTA. Our treatment under the classical hypothesis gets around this debate by treating all the regions symmetrically, cutting taxes and tariffs equally for all.

One can work on the classical hypothesis in two ways. Say's Law prescribes liberalizing only the supply side of the market. This is consistent with easing up such domestic taxes as a value added or goods and service tax on output produced at home for domestic and foreign consumption. As we show, such taxes were increasing recently, albeit at less than 1 percent per year. But one also has to liberalize trade, which involves dropping not only export but import taxes as well. So, liberalization in the classical method involves working with both blades of the scissors, namely supply and demand.

> **Hypothesis 2:** [Keynesian]: *In choosing economic policies, a country gives first preference to achieving domestic equilibrium, leaving the foreign sector to adjust accordingly.*

John Maynard Keynes has made the argument that one should undertake policies at home to steer the domestic economy, and let the international sector adjust accordingly. To be faithful to this argument, we will protect domestic output with a 10 percent tax hike on output, while doing a 10 percent liberalization on export and import tariffs. This hypothesis in part hedges the risk of some liberalization by trading off some increase taxes from domestic output for the liberalization of the external sector. If liberalization of trade is beneficial then a country can begin the policy experiment of dropping domestic taxes on output, thereby, in the limit, liberalizing both their internal and external sectors over time. In this sense, the classical hypothesis is a limiting case of the Keynesian hypothesis.

To model tax hikes within liberalization schema requires some justifications that output taxes have been increasing. Table 5.1 indicates that the tax rates on output have increased slightly from 2009 to 2011. The International Publishers Association (IPA) has put out two surveys on VAT (Value Added Tax) and GST (Goods and Service Tax) in 2009 and 2011. (IPA, 2009, 2011, *Global Survey on Books & Electronics*: http://www.internationalpublishers.org). Of the 88 countries surveyed, the tax rates for the Triad regions remained fairly stable, as indicated in Table 6.1. Note that only Canada has reported data in the IPA survey for the NAM region. The tax rates average approximately 20, 10, 5, and 15 percent for Europe, Asian, NAM, and RoW, respectively. The less than a percent change for the region displayed in Part A of the table may reflect policymakers' desire to avoid taxation in a current recessionary period. In Part B, we see an indication that the emphasis on no reduced rates has shifted from paperbacks to e-books. The emphasis for reduced rate shows the opposite tendency, from e-books to paperbacks.

TABLE 6.1 *Triad VAT and GST tax rates in percent*

Part A

	Percentage VAT/GST			Range: both surveys		Countries with maximum tax rates
	2009	2011	Change	Minimum	Maximum	
Europe	19.32	20.16	0.84	8	25.00	Denmark, Iceland, Norway, Sweden
Asia	9.87	10	0.13	1.5	17.00	China and Pakistan
NAM	5.00	5	0.00	5	5.00	Canada
RoW	14.94	15.11	0.17	5	22.00	Uruguay

Part B

	Number of countries			
	Survey 2009		Survey 2011	
	Paperback	E-books	Paperback	E-books
Exemption for all	6	15	14	7
Reduced rates for all	3	33	32	3
Reduced rates or exemption	18	26	31	27
No reduced rate or exemptions	51	13	11	39
Treatment not known	10	1	0	12
Sample size (number of countries)	88	88	88	88

Note: Only Canada Reported for the NAFTA area.
Source: Tabulated form IPA (2009, 2011) surveys.

Trends in the PPI

Table 6.2 displays trends in the PPI. The years 1995 and 2000 in the sample are milestones dates, the former marking the year after NAFTA was formed, and the latter being one year after the EMU adopted the EURO currency. Within the 1995–2000 time interval, the Asian economies suffered their high-tech balance of payment crises, starting with the devaluation of Thailand's baht in July 1997.

In Table 6.2, one cannot miss the point that the annual percent trade of the PPI in the EU is approximately double that of North America, and more than five times that of Asia and RoW. Trading for the PPI is fairly flat throughout the sample period, except for a little blip in the aftermath of the EMU for the years 2000 and 2001. While the share of North America is a discernible decreasing trend from 1995 to 2009, the shares for Asia and RoW increased slightly.

Computational general equilibrium (CGE) analysis

We now turn to modeling the PPI data from a CGE point of view. For this purpose, we have adopted the Triad regions discussed along with RoW, which gives us four regions. Trading sectors are reduced to flows

TABLE 6.2 *Historic trade trends ($ths dollars) in the PPI*

Year	Asia	%	NAM	%	Europe	%	RoW	%	Total
1993	12,627	8.39	41,619	27.64	82,400	54.73	13,905	9.24	150,551
1994	11,830	8.67	36,490	26.74	76,185	55.82	11,971	8.77	136,476
1995	12,342	9.26	36,296	27.23	72,997	54.77	11,650	8.74	133,285
1998	13,451	9.83	35,528	25.96	75,671	55.29	12,219	8.93	136,869
1999	14,657	10.63	36,309	26.34	74,826	54.28	12,056	8.75	137,848
2000	17,254	11.61	41,374	27.84	75,602	50.87	14,395	9.69	148,625
2001	17,191	11.79	38,647	26.50	75,646	51.87	14,340	9.83	145,824
2002	17,384	11.90	36,206	24.78	78,956	54.03	13,579	9.29	146,125
2003	19,211	11.46	38,748	23.11	92,435	55.12	17,300	10.32	167,694
2004	22,444	11.98	42,532	22.70	103,332	55.16	19,022	10.15	187,330
2005	24,627	12.46	45,071	22.80	106,363	53.81	21,595	10.93	197,656
2006	27,441	12.95	47,310	22.32	114,413	53.98	22,786	10.75	211,950
2007	34,135	14.55	47,968	20.45	126,853	54.07	25,643	10.93	234,599
2008	38,015	14.16	51,449	19.16	148,301	55.23	30,768	11.46	268,533
2009	34,747	15.48	41,763	18.61	122,029	54.38	25,874	11.53	224,413

Source: Compiled from GTAP Eight Time Series Data Base, 1995–2009 ($ths.)

of printing and publishing, food, manufacturing, textile, mining, and others, or six sectors. In the parlance of CGE analysis, we will be analyzing a 4 × 6 model, that is, four regions and six sectors.

The details of the CGE model are described in Hertel's 1997 book. We are able to estimate welfare benefits from trading in the PPI industry globally. The benefits follow from regions competing in order to increase their world share of the market. A region can improve its benefits in three important ways. First, a region can have a policy of taxing the output or income of nonsaving commodities to improve its allocative efficiency. Second, it can benefit from terms of trade policies. Third, it can improve its policy mix with a view of free trade in mind.

Table 6.3 displays the results for the CGE analysis of the 4 × 6 regional-sector model described in the introduction. The first five columns are results for the Classical hypothesis, while the next five columns are results for the Keynesian hypothesis. From the classical point of view, 1997 was a year of positive welfare benefits following the 100 percent liberation of its internal and external sectors. As the "total" column indicates, under the Classical hypothesis, the world gained $314.34 million in 1997 from liberalization of the PPI sector. This is a result of the import liberalization bringing in $4,480.29 million that compensated for the loss of $324.96 million in output tax, and $3,840.91 in export tax losses. Similar analysis for the years 2001 and 2007 indicate that import liberalization did not bring in as much gain to cover losses from output and export subsidies, indicating that the world lost from liberalization in those years. In large part, trends in liberalization for the classical hypothesis for 1997, 2001, and 2007 reflect some convergence among global trading in the PPI, eliminating the gains from differences due to factor prices, which are becoming more equalized across the regions.

The results of the Keynesian hypothesis, listed in the last five columns of Table 6.3, show positive world benefits for all years. World benefits increased from $96.43 million in 1997 to $189.45 in 2001 and $2,099.84 in 2007. Both output taxes and import liberalization contributed to those increased benefits. The year 2007 is the event horizon of the Great Recession, which marks the contribution of import and output liberalization. No doubt technology was a driving force behind the expansion, as reflected in increased output due to upward drifts in countries' production function.

One perceptible trend is that NAM and EU did much better under the Classical than under the Keynesian hypothesis. They gained while Asia

TABLE 6.3 CGE benefits due to improved allocation and policy mixes

	100% liberation of TO, TXS, TMS					10% tax hike at home and 10% liberalization of trade				
Regions	Total	Output	Export	Import	Regions	Total	Output	Export	Import
Results for year 2007 ($m)									
NAM	24,713.98	15,931.07	4,924.51	3,858.4	NAFTA	−714.82	−1,593.11	492.45	385.84
EU_25	39,470.74	15,754.84	19,155.98	4,559.92	EU_25	796.11	−1,575.48	1,915.6	455.99
ASIA	−28,004	−17,469.3	−9,080.84	−1,453.82	ASIA	693.47	1,746.93	−908.08	−145.38
RoW	−55,415.6	−34,333.2	−23949.5	2,867.13	RoW	1,325.08	3,433.32	−2,394.95	286.71
Total	−19,234.8	−20,116.6	−8949.85	9,831.63		2,099.84	2,011.66	−894.98	983.16
	GTAP	TO	TMS	TXS			TO	TXS	TMS
Results for year 2001 ($m)									
NAM	23,752.16	16,572.89	5,125.66	2,053.61	NAFTA	−939.36	−1,657.29	512.57	205.36
EU_25	20,977.26	12,620.84	7,501.21	855.21	EU_25	−426.44	−1,262.08	750.12	85.52
ASIA	−24,718.4	−16,916.5	−6,538.02	−1,263.89	ASIA	911.45	1,691.64	−653.8	−126.39
RoW	−20,523.1	−13,480.5	−11,221.7	4,179.16	RoW	643.8	1,348.05	−1122.17	417.92
Total	−512.04	−1,203.26	−5,132.87	5,824.09		189.45	120.32	−513.28	582.41
Results for year 1997 ($m)									
NAM	36,062.8	22,743.63	9,399.54	3,919.63	NAFTA	−942.45	−2,274.36	939.95	391.96
EU_25	28,083.86	17,221.44	9,264.16	1,598.24	EU_25	−635.9	−1,722.14	926.42	159.82
ASIA	−34,134.2	−22,735.3	−9,289.64	−2,109.24	ASIA	1,133.64	2,273.53	−928.96	−210.92
RoW	−29,698	−17,554.7	−13,215	1,071.66	RoW	541.14	1,755.47	−1321.5	107.17
Total	314.43	−324.96	−3,840.91	4,480.29		96.43	32.5	−384.09	448.03

Source: 2007 Gtap8; 2004 Gtap8; 2001 Gtap6, and 1997 Gtap5.4 Data Bases.

and RoW lost from 100 percent internal and external liberalization. One easy explanation for this is that liberalization is more favorable to developed than underdeveloped economies. It is now well documented in economic history that export substitution was going on in the undeveloped nations in the latter half of the 20th century, driving them to core periphery theory and export substitution regimes during the sample period. When the Former Soviet Union (FSU) failed, many FSU countries became members of the EMU, and other underdeveloped nations began to embrace capitalism.

We must now delve into the aggregated results of Table 6.4 in order to discern the performance of major players in the region. The Triad regional classification has China and India in Asia; Russia in RoW; UK, France, and Germany in EU; and United States in NAM. Some analysis of the PPI for these major players in the Triad regions seems warranted.

Table 6.4 displays the value and annual share for major countries in the Triad regions. The data indicate that North America, United States, and Canada were equal in PPI share participation in trade in 1995. While United States's share increased in 1997 over Canada's share, the NAFTA countries' share started a decline in 2001, with United States and Mexico's shares recovering in 2009.

Table 6.4 also shows that China's share of the Asian market began to dominate the Asian region in 2001. As Japan displayed a stable trend of approximately 2 percent for the sample periods, and India's share remained somewhat stable at less than half of a percent, the gain in China's share is from other countries in that region. The slight decline in shares between 1997 and 2001 for China and Japan might be a result of the Financial Crisis in the Asia-Pacific Area in 1998.

In the EU region, Germany's share of the PPI is slightly greater than that of France and Great Britain combined. Germany's share remained stable in 1995 and 1997, but started to increase from 2007 onward, while that of France and Great Britain fell slightly throughout the period. The shares of the major countries in the RoW sector for the PPI are indeed small.

Germany

As Table 6.4 indicates, the largest share in the world market of the PPI industry is in Germany, which had almost 13 percent in 2009, versus 11 percent in the United States, and 7 percent in Canada. Strong market

TABLE 6.4 PPI for major countries in the Triad regions

Areas	1995	%	1997	%	2001	%	2007	%	2008	%	2009	%
Major countries in the North America												
United States	20,575	13.67	19,064	14.30	19,280	13.22	26,262	11.19	29,357	10.93	24,953	11.12
Canada	20,356	13.52	16,428	12.33	18,354	12.59	19,912	8.49	20,292	7.56	15,210	6.78
Mexico	688	0.46	804	0.60	1,013	0.69	1,794	0.76	1,798	0.67	1,599	0.71
Major countries in Asia												
China	1,618	1.07	1,725	1.29	3243	2.22	11,378	4.85	13,297	4.95	12,560	5.60
Japan	2,854	1.90	2,483	1.86	2,600	1.78	4,236	1.81	4,845	1.80	4,175	1.86
India	174	0.12	127	0.10	292	0.20	751	0.32	983	0.37	888	0.40
Major countries in EU												
Germany	17,809	11.83	14,943	11.21	15795	10.83	29,563	12.60	34,057	12.68	28,406	12.66
France	8,326	5.53	7,341	5.51	7,446	5.11	11,192	4.77	12,319	4.59	10,245	4.57
United Kingdom	6,881	4.57	7,174	5.38	6,137	4.21	9,346	3.98	10,009	3.73	8,334	3.71
Major Countries in RoW												
Brazil	2,741	1.82	2,111	1.58	2438	1.67	4553	1.94	6559	2.44	5504	2.45
Venezuela	150	0.10	165	0.12	76	0.05	12	0.01	13	0.00	4	0.00
Russia	1,738	1.15	1,687	1.27	2193	1.50	3393	1.45	3670	1.37	2878	1.28
RoW	66,641	44.26	59,233	44.44	66957	45.92	112207	47.83	131334	48.91	109657	48.86
Total	150,551		133,285		145824		234599		268533		224413	

Source: GTAP8 Data ($m).

share rivalry seems to be present between the United States, Canada, and Germany over the sample periods since 1995. The historic record shows that in 1910, Germany had 31,281 book titles published, relative to 13,470 in the United States, 12,615 in France, and 10,804 in England. On the eve of World War I, Germany's dominant position remained intact with 34,871 titles published in 1913 (Tatlock, 2010, p. 4).

Germany had a comparative advantage in scientific publishing in the first half of the 20th century (Sarkowski, 2001). From 1918 to 1933, a third of the world Nobel Prizes in Physics, Chemistry, and Medicine were awarded to German scientists (ibid., p. 28). By the time of Germany's surrender in May 8, 1945, the four-zone division of the country made it difficult for the book industry to function. Leipzig, the regional center of publishing activities, was practically destroyed. Germany was prevented from engaging in export activities for a time, but resumed in the 1950s. Meanwhile, US companies were reprinting German volumes and selling them at lower world prices. Springer-Verlag lost some 894 scientific volumes to the US firm J.W. Edwards in 1943 and 1944, but began overseas operations in the 1950s and 1960s (ibid., p. 31).

In recent years, Germany's share of the e-book market is a small 1 percent of its book industry, relative to 20.2 percent in the United States in 2011(*Business Week*, April 29, 2012). The difference is largely attributable to cultural preferences, and perhaps to the historic legacy of the invention of the printing press in Germany.

China

Table 6.4 indicates that since 2001, China has overtaken Japan as the leader of PPI activities in the Asian region. China has approximately 15,800 business directed to consumers (B-2-C) and consumer to consumer (C-2-C) book companies online. China's leading position in the region started in 1999 with the formation of Dangdang Inc, a B-2-C online entity. By December 2011, Dangdang offered approximately 50,000 e-book titles. Jingdong.com is a major rival of Dangdang Inc., currently offering approximately 80,000 e-book titles. Dangdang Inc. and Jindong.com offer approximately 300,000, and 200,000 physical book titles, respectively (Ostapenko, 2012, pp. 2–4).

TAA subsidies

Trade Adjustment Assistance (TAA) subsidies, meant to provide relief to the US publishing industry, were not large enough to be effective. The information in Table 6.5 indicates that during the immediate post-NAFTA period, TAA was geared up for negative import impacts from Mexico and Canada. Subsequently, countries for the Asian Triad became its focus.

Future of the Triad region

The United States holds the leadership position in governance and technology in the PPI industry that initiated development in North America, Europe, Asia, and RoW since the 1940s. Japan became a big player in the IT network and hardware in the 1980s, and Europe developed its mobile network in the 1990s (Cowhey and Aronson, 2009, p. 97). Now India and China are capitalizing on these development more than any other developing countries.

Table 6.6 illustrates the share of the Triad region. As it indicates, North America has the largest share of spending, followed by Europe and then

TABLE 6.5   TAA certification and denial

	Certified		Denied		
Year	Petitions	Workers	Petitions	Workers	Countries that impacted certification
1996	2	1,200	2	234	Mexico and Canada
1997	2	370	5	289	Mexico
1998	0	130	0	0	NA
1999	1	27	5	950	NA
2000	1	260	0	0	NA
2001	4	245	1	80	NA
2002	7	332	4	489	NA
2003	3	61	1	4	China
2004	0	0	1	143	NA
2005	4	389	1	44	NA
2006	1	22	0	0	NA
2007	7	210	0	0	India, Malaysia, Italy, China, South Korea, Phillipines, Spain
2008	14	475	0	0	India, Mexico, Phillipines

Source: Compiled from www.citizen.org/taadatabase.

TABLE 6.6 *Global computer market information and communication technology (ICT) spending*

Regions	2000 %	2005 %	2009 %
NAM	47.75	41.36	
Europe	27.96	32.3	
Asia	21.31	21.39	28.8
RoW	2.98	4.95	
Total	100	100	

Source: World Information Technology and Service Alliance (WITSA) *Digital Planet* Reports (2004, 2005, 2010).

Asia. *Digital Planet 2010* reported that the recession created a 3 percent decline in ICT spending globally in 2009, with North America declining by 4.4 percent and Europe by 6.6 percent, and Asia gaining by 2.4 percent (WITSA *Digital Planet*, October 2010 Executive Summary, p. 14). All the Triad regions are expected to recover by 2013, but at varying rates.

Conclusion

The PPI industry within the Triad regions of the global economy has been examined from the classical and Keynesian economic points of view. While the world gained from 100 percent liberalization of its internal and external sectors, it appears that factor price equalization may have occurred in the current state of the economy. Benefits from some protection are now in vogue, underscoring the strength of the Keynesian hypothesis.

The big players in the Triad regions are Germany in the EU, United States in North America, and China in Asia. Germany seems to be lagging in its e-book efforts, an area that the United States currently leads, and into which China is rapidly expanding. Germany's hesitancy to enter the e-book market may be partly based on its cultural preference for brick-and-mortar bookstores. TAA subsidies continue to be too small to enable global competition in the industry.

7
Internet Technological Aspects of the Industry

Abstract: *Books possess inherent characteristics that make them a natural product to buy and sell online. They are easy to ship, inexpensive to warehouse and inventory, easy to review and rate, can be test read, and can easily be searched. The Internet provides a widened audience with low-cost, 24-hour access to a diverse world of selections. The Internet is the battlefield at the conjunction of production, consumption, and distribution, and has become more and more competitive for book publishers. The Internet has made value chains more efficient, particularly in the area of digitized books, where digital information is available to intermediaries who produce books from the digital copies. Accounting records are kept of various sales transactions by region, creating a source of information economies.*

Ramrattan, Lall, and Michael Szenberg. *Revolutions in Book Publishing: The Effects of Digital Innovation on the Industry*. New York: Palgrave Macmillan, 2016.
DOI: 10.1057/9781137576217.0012.

Introduction

Books have distinguishing characteristics that makes them great candidates for online sales. They are inexpensive, varied, easy to ship, cheap to warehouse and inventory, easy to review and rate, can be test read, and can be easily searched (Morgan-Stanley, 1997, pp. 8-2, 8-3). We may also emphasize the advantages of the Internet that are compatible with book selling, including its "wide reach, exhaustive product selection, little infrastructure requirement, unlimited opening hours, and a high degree of scalability" (Enders and Jelassi, 2000, pp. 543-544).

Technological innovation has put the book industry on the Internet. David Ricardo, the famous classical economist, argued in his principles that machinery tends to enhance profits and rents. Joseph Schumpeter placed innovation at the heart of modern competition, where new products must be continuously invented to replace old ones in a creative destruction process. The new digital information age or Information Technology (IT) revolution is a movement toward wetware, away from the traditional hardware and software emphasis for growth. Paul Romer, a leading modern growth theorist, explains that Wetware is based on the new combination of intangibles of a company or country, developing better formulas for creating value (Romer, 1998, p. 11). One expects the Internet to be profitable for businesses while also making gains for consumers, in the way that all successful technological innovations have done in the past. The purpose of this chapter is to appraise that aspect of the Internet for the book industry.

The Internet presents many opportunities and possibilities for making profit. Enhancement of profits can come from both the revenue and cost sides of the profit equation. On the revenue side, IT allows sellers to reach a broader market and gain advantages for providing superior services to customers. On the cost side, production processes can be split into stages that can be separated in space locally and globally for outsourcing and off-shoring activities (Helpman, 2011, pp. 126-127). For instance, the production of a book does not have to take place entirely within a single manufacturing facility, and a company may find it cheaper to outsource the typesetting, for example, to a foreign country. The authors' 2007 book *Franco Modigliani*, part of UK publisher Palgrave Macmillan's Great Thinkers series, was edited and typeset in India; technology has allowed the company to tap into lower-cost foreign labor without any delay.

Google's Book Search initiative has presented the book industry with a paradigm shift. Digital technology has allowed millions of books to be scanned and made available to institutions and readers. This makes booksellers fear for the future, and in fact Google was sued by the Authors Guild and Association of American Publishers when the Book Search project began in 2005. A settlement was reached, allowing Google to create a market for out-of-print books.

The book industry's challenge has been to expand, extend, and adapt to the many new possibilities offered by the Internet. The industry tends to adapt in stages, with remarkable success at first, followed by many stumbling blocks. We will use the law of economics to appraise the industry's structure, conduct, and performance with regard to new technology. For the purpose of laying out the relevant background information of the Internet for the book industry, we will follow the chart outline in Figure 7.1. The figure gives an overview of what we observe happening in the book publishing industry following the Internet revolution.

Internet technology

Figure 7.1 indicates how changes in communication and computer technology characterize the new Informational Technology (IT) revolution. IT stands with the inventions of canals, railroads, and the automobile as a major engine of sustained growth for the economy. Since the 1940s, IT has evolved from analogue to digital technology, creating a digital economy that forever altered "characteristics of information, computing, and communication" (Brynjolfsson and Kahin, 2002, p. 1). But more importantly, IT has brought together communication technology (which has shifted from radio to satellite-based technology), and computer technology (which has moved from general purpose to biotech and ultra-intelligent computers) (Dicken, 2007, p. 78). The final result is a revolutionary way of doing business in a digital economy.

When the Internet began, it relied on existing telephone companies to form the backbone of transmission through their telephone lines. Prior to April 1995, the Internet was in the hands of a few institutional researchers. Its original backbone was ARPANET (Advance Research Project Agency of the Department of Defense). Then the National Science Foundation, NSFNET, entered the picture. By 1995, NSFNET's involvement was over, and it was replaced with a commercial backbone,

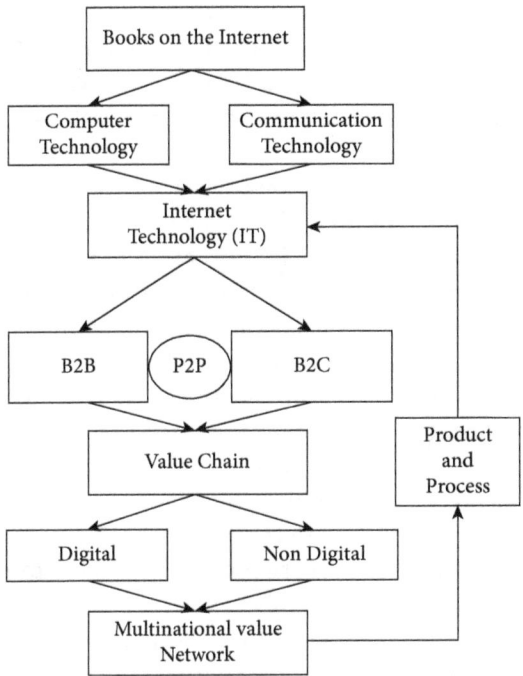

FIGURE 7.1   Outline of issues in Internet technology

marking the privatization of the Internet. In 1997, the Clinton administration published *A Framework for Global Electronic Commerce*, emphasizing five points:

1   The private sector should lead.
2   Governments should avoid undue restrictions on electronic commerce.
3   Where governmental involvement is needed, its aim should be to support and enforce a predictable, minimalist, consistent, and simple legal environment for commerce.
4   Governments should recognize the unique qualities of the Internet. The genius and explosive success of the Internet can be attributed in part to its decentralized nature and to its tradition of bottom-up governance.
5   Electronic commerce on the Internet should be facilitated on a global basis.

These points form the foundation for the more modern developments of Transmission Control Protocol/Internet Protocol (TCP-IP); e-mail, File Transfer Protocol (FTP), and the World Wide Web (see David, 2001), which enable the book industry and other industries to flourish on the Internet.

The modern Internet Backbone Providers (IBP) allow customers to connect with other end users through Internet Service Providers (ISP). Metaphorically, a model for this interconnection can be a consumer in the Atlantic Ocean wanting to connect with a customer in the Pacific Ocean. Assume the two oceans are two backbones. We can call the Panama Canal a point of interconnection (POI). When a customer in San Francisco wants to connect with one in Los Angeles, he will use only the Pacific backbone, which we call on-network traffic. If the San Francisco customer wishes to connect with a customer in New York, then the traffic will go through the POI, resulting in off-network traffic. The implication of this framework for benefit to consumers, quality of service, and investment for the future of the Internet can be modeled in various ways. To allow off-network traffic, the IBPs pay each other settlement or termination charges that are set above the marginal cost of terminating calls, making IBPs monopoly operators (Laffront and Tirole, 2002, p. 179).

Prior to the 1970s, the backbone was monopolized by AT&T. During the 1970s, MCI and Sprint began to break up this monopoly. As of 2010, the number of long-distance service providers grew to approximately 1,900. Service providers are regulated by the FCC, which tends to favor competition rather than regulation (FCC, 2010, p. 9–1). Table 7.1 shows the top five IBP players dominating the amount of toll revenues, even though the percent of revenues fell somewhat, from 74.39 to 61.88 percent, between 2000 and 2008.

The rights of IBP companies, such as intellectual property rights, patents, and ownership of specific assets, form a source of their monopoly power. A more important aspect, however, is not just holding rights, but the ability of large companies to bear the costs of developing rights into innovations. Book firms such as Amazon and Barnes & Noble have to hook up to the backbone companies via ISPs and other providers, and are therefore subject to the monopoly prices for their services. A dissertation by Mortimer found that congestion and network reliability provides incentives for IBPs to interconnect. IBP's market share correlates with congestion, creating incentives for further investments (Mortimer, 2001, p. 103).

TABLE 7.1 *Five firms' share of toll revenues*

Year	Five companies that report the most toll service revenue	Five companies' revenues ($m)	Total revenues ($m)	%
2000	AT&T Communications; Qwest Services Corp.; SBC Communications, Inc.; Sprint Corp.; WorldCom, Inc.	81,546	109,615	74.39
2001	AT&T Communications; SBC Communications, Inc.; Sprint Corp.; Verizon Communications, Inc.; WorldCom, Inc.	73,486	99,053	74.19
2002	AT&T Communications; SBC Communications, Inc.; Sprint Corp.; Verizon Communications, Inc.; WorldCom, Inc.	59,864	83,697	71.52
2003	AT&T Communications; MCI, Inc.; SBC Communications, Inc.; Sprint Corp.; Verizon Communications, Inc.	52,172	77,188	67.59
2004	AT&T Corp.; SBC Communications, Inc.; Sprint Corporation; Verizon Communications Inc.; WorldCom, Inc.	46,511	71,214	65.31
2005	AT&T, Inc.; Qwest Services Corp.; SBC Long Distance, LLC; Sprint Nextel Corporation; Verizon Communications, Inc.	46,599	69,250	67.29
2006	AT&T Inc.; Level 3 Financing, Inc.; Qwest Services Corp.; Sprint Nextel Corporation; Verizon Communications, Inc.	45,015	64,379	69.92
2007	AT&T, Inc; Level 3 Financing, Inc.; Qwest Services Corp.; Sprint Nextel Corporation; Verizon Communications, Inc.	42,907	64,802	66.21
2008	AT&T, Inc; Level 3 Financing, Inc.; Qwest Services Corp.; Sprint Nextel Corporation; Verizon Communications, Inc.	37,070	59,910	61.88

Source: FCC (2010).

Book industry players on the Internet

Figure 7.1 also indicates how competition in the book industry is played out on the Internet. The players in the book industry on the Internet represent extension and addition to the traditional brick-and-mortar book industry. The players are still (1) The buyers, who are residents and businesses; (2) The firm, publishers or booksellers, who now have websites; and (3) A large group of intermediary players who are distributors, wholesalers, retailers, and providers of advice on what products to buy and where to buy them.

Competition among the players is viewed in light of a value chain. On the Internet, the value chain is a multinational network of activities that link primary activities (production, marketing, delivery, and servicing) with supportive activities (technology, human resources, procurement, and inputs in general) (Porter, 1990, pp. 40–41). The value chain concept, developed by Michael Porter, is driven by profits measured as the difference between what the buyer is willing to pay for the product or service, less the cost of all activities the firm engaged in to produce the product (ibid., p. 40). In 1999, the Census Bureau's Printing and Publishing report announced that "an explosion of Internet activity has enlarged the sphere of international contacts for U. S. publishers, further expanding global markets for U. S. books" (Printing and Publishing, 1999, p. 15).

The overarching philosophy of a book industry value chain on the Internet is to please the customer. Consumer sovereignty has led some observers to argue that the value chain has transformed emphasis from book-to-business (B2B) model to a new business-to-consumer (B2C) model, as indicated in Figure 7.1 (Smith, Bailey, and Brynjolfsson, 2002, p. 123). One incarnation of consumer sovereignty has been peer-to-peer (P2P) sharing of files. Gayer and Shy (2003, 198) have modeled P2P markets for digital products on a continuum, where customers can buy a product in a store or download it from a digital file on the Internet. Such a market can be fully defined, where the whole [0, 1] interval is partitioned into buying on the Internet or buying in-store, or only partially defined, where the interval is partitioned into buying on the Internet, buying in-store, or do not buy. This type of modeling represents extreme cases where marginal cost tends to be insignificant or zero. The experience was demonstrated by the now defunct Napster, which used P2P file sharing technology that has since morphed into other forms now such as GNU and FreeNet technologies (Ghosemajumder, 2002, p. 2). The proliferation of free books on the web is a good case where MC tends to zero. The numerous combinations of business models for the book industry on the Internet can be conceptualized from an arrangement such as the one demonstrated in Figure 7.2.

Figure 7.2 illustrates the possibilities of a vertical value chain between producers and consumers. The value chain in the digital world of books starts with the publisher or producer, who makes the digital information available to intermediaries. Some would define the essence of information as digitization (Shapiro and Varian, 1999, p. 3). Books are then produced from the digital copies. Accounting records are kept of various sales transactions by region and by customer, creating a source of information economies.

The value chain, as outlined in Figure 7.2, operates for both the digital and nondigital worlds. In a nondigital world where the physical book is involved, the value chain moves among distributors, wholesalers, retailers, and shippers. For instance, Barnes & Noble and Amazon.com will ship a book from their inventory, or forward an order to an authorized seller, using e-mail to confirm the transaction. In 1999, for instance, Amazon.com increased its warehousing capacities by tenfold from the previous year, adding seven warehouses in the United States, one in the United Kingdom and one in Germany. Amazon was poised for rapid growth and competition in providing quick and reliable services to the customers (Enders and Jelassi, 2000, p. 548). Such activities employ back-end integration for warehousing and shipping and front-end integration of physical stores and in-store services, as indicated in Figure 7.2 (ibid., 2000, p. 547).

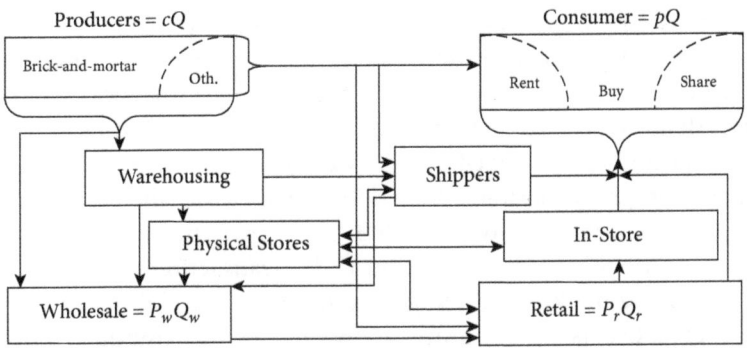

FIGURE 7.2 *Book industry value chain: business to consumer*

Figure 7.2 also demonstrates a vertically integrated chain, as described, for instance, by Brynjolfsson, Hu, and Smith (2003). We enter Figure 7.2 in the northwest quadrant, where the publisher produces a quantity, Q, at a marginal cost of c. The publisher can reach the retailer either directly or through the wholesaler/distributor. The wholesale price, P_w, is usually a large discount (43–51 percent) off the list price set by the publisher. The retail tends to be the same as the wholesale price, $p_r = p_w$, if the retailer gets the book from the wholesaler, or equal to discount from the list price if the retailer gets the book from the publisher. This model does exclude cases where consumers can special-order a book directly from the publisher. The formulation of this vertically integrated chain supports easy calculation of profits as revenues less costs, consumer surplus from trading on the Internet, and welfare benefits (ibid., 2003).

Some elaborations of the costs implied in Figure 7.2 are in order. Producer costs are traditionally fixed and are variable. Set up costs include those necessary for firms entering the market. Firms can select a basic level of service costs for administration, websites, and distributions to minimize costs. Endogenous fixed costs go beyond the basic level costs, to include quality of service, speed, security, advertising: in short, costs that allow the book industry firms to strategize (Latcovich and Smith, 2001, p. 220). The cost variable, c, in Figure 7.2 can be thought of as the marginal cost of the producer. On the Internet, marginal cost can be very insignificant, and the same is true for warehousing costs in digital form. For instance, one source reported that the cost of storage for a 320-page book, about a megabyte of data, fell from $5,000 to around 17 cents in the period 1975–1999 (Carlsson, 2004, p. 255).

The consumer block in Figure 7.2 is partitioned to consider markets where consumers can buy, share, or rent a book (Varian, 2000b). The producer is a monopolist who wants to maximize profit = revenues − costs. Revenue is calculated by ranking the consumers' willingness to read a book. The willingness of the yth consumer to pay for reading a book is denoted $r(y)$, so that revenues will be $r(y)y$. The producer incurs a marginal cost, c, and a fixed cost, F (Varian, 2000b, p. 475).

As an example of sharing, Varian considered a case where a consumer can read a book as a member of a club. There are k members of the club, x copies of a book available to them and a transaction cost, t, such as waiting for the book or traveling cost to attend the club meeting. The seller's objective is to minimize members' cost of reading. When a consumer buys a book, the marginal cost is c. When the consumer shares the book, the cost is split equally among k consumers, or c/k. Comparing the cost of sharing, $c/k + t$ with the cost of buying, c, reveals some salient facts. Assume the cost of sharing is less than the cost of buying; then $(t < c - ck = c)k -1$. In that case, if a library is available, more reading will take place, price per read will be minimized, profits maximized, and consumers will be better off (ibid., p. 476).

In addition to buying and sharing, consumers now have the option of renting books, although the selection of books is currently limited. In his article, Varian discussed other facts from the consumer side about sharing/renting and buying/renting, and from the producer side about selling/renting and pricing to buy versus pricing to rent. The value of renting a book can be compared to the utility of buying or sharing a book. For instance, if the book is used only a single time, then the value of renting is the same as the value of owning. If $u_b - c \geq u_r - b/k - t$, where u_b, u_r are the utilities of buying and renting, respectively, b is the price of buying, and k,t are defined as above, then buying is preferred over renting.

The last block of Figure 7.1 emphasizes that the book industry is a multinational network. Multinational network activities were revolutionized several times in history, notably during the time of Columbus, prior to World War I, and presently. The present stage is characterized by *increased speed and volume* in the movement of goods and messages; *shrinking space* (instantaneous telecommunications); *permeable borders* (pollution and capital mobility); *reflexivity* (people are local and global in behavior; and *risk and trust* (Mad Cow Disease, spread of AIDS) (Beynon and Dunkerley, 2000, pp. 5–6). More importantly, the present stage is marked by the Internet technology that is constantly still evolving.

The ability to store books in digital form has created demand for electronic ways to read, including hand-held devices such as the iPad and Kindle. Digital technology also allows consumers to print, bind, and trim a copy of a book on demand. College textbooks and readers can now be customized to meet different course requirements.

As Internet technology evolves, a feedback loop develops between the multinational Network block to the top of Figure 7.1, accounting for product and process innovation in the book industry. Process innovation allows print-on-demand and versioning. Traditionally, book sellers had to carry a large inventory, which carried enormous costs, especially if the book did not sell well and had to be returned. Digital storage and print-on-demand lessen that burden (Greco, 2005, p. 176). Producers are able to offer hardcover and paperback editions, professional and popular versions, low priced versus high priced versions (Varian, 2000a, p. 138).

Conclusion

This chapter appraises the still budding aspects of the book industry on the Internet. The Internet firms strive for perpetual innovation in Internet retailing. By expanding into broader product groups, fostering a network of independent merchants, and offering low shipping, Amazon was able to stem the tide of the recent recession. We see that ISPs and IBPs that service the Internet are modeled as imperfect competition, which may occasion dominant firms such as Amazon and Barnes & Noble.

Conclusions

Abstract: *The production side of the industry picks up on the pervasiveness of technological advances. As new technology diffuses across the domestic and global industry, production with increasing returns is realized. We see competition among dominant firms such as Amazon, Barnes & Noble, and Books-a-Million. As expected, these large firms prevent their competitors from instituting policies that would cut into their market share. The book industry will not disappear—humanity would not survive without the written word. However, it remains to be seen what form those words will take. The structure of the book industry will continue to evolve along with the technologies that shape it and propel it forward.*

Ramrattan, Lall, and Michael Szenberg. *Revolutions in Book Publishing: The Effects of Digital Innovation on the Industry.* New York: Palgrave Macmillan, 2016.
DOI: 10.1057/9781137576217.0013.

Online bookselling and publishing have revolutionized the printing and publishing industry, shifting it away from the traditional mode of business and forcing it to keep pace with the trends and cycles of the Internet Communication and Technology sectors. Even in Germany, whose printing legacy is so historically entrenched, the PPI cannot resist the lure of expanding online.

Demand and supply tools highlight the new parametric structure of the book industry, and can still internalize the dynamic changes in the industry. Demand has been extended to include human capital formation and search procedures. Supply now integrates the publisher versus bookseller gaming aspect of the market. The market comes together in a dynamic programming way. We find that firms can fix prices for a long time, indicating some market power. For instance, Amazon has standardized some book prices on the Internet, without much consequence of retaliation from rivals.

Price and quantity snapshots at a point in time reflect expectations of changing technology. The current expectation of future innovation will determine winners and losers. The digital wave of innovation continues to dominate as technology adapts to fill niches in demand. This is becoming prominent in the various ways books are now being read on e-reader devices, the rising cost of college textbooks, and the expectation that college texts must adapt to students' needs. Libraries are also impacted by the switch to low-cost data and e-books, which provide a viable alternative to the high cost of shelving and managing books.

While the United States maintains a dominant share of the ICT market, its rivals from the Triad regions—North America, Europe, and Asia—are in perpetual motion. In particular, China is rapidly expanding its domestic book market, pushing Asia into a dominant role in the global market. Any technological complacency on the part of the members of the Triad region will be at the peril of losing substantial market share in the future.

The production side of the industry picks up on the pervasiveness of technological advances. As new technology diffuses across the domestic and global industry, production with increasing returns is realized. We see competition among dominant firms such as Amazon, Barnes & Noble, and Books-a-Million. As expected, these large firms prevent their competitors from instituting policies that would cut into their market share. When Amazon, for instance, pioneered the use of the Internet for book sales, its rivals reacted with their own net servers. When one firm differentiates itself with discounts and service strategies, the others follow. But the market has not yet settled. The exits of Borders Books and other publishing enterprises show that larger operations that are complacent will suffer. Independent sellers are struggling to find their place in the market.

In the distribution section, we examined two major hypotheses, one by Joe Bain regarding firm size and concentration, and the other by Joseph Stiglitz regarding firm size and rewards. The fact that there are few large firms in the industry does not mean that small firms do not fill a valuable role. For instance, small firms can carve out a market share based on the quality of the books they produce. Rewards tend to be tied to productivity. The industry, however, has shown an increase in the four-firm concentration ratios. Declining trends were also observed in the industry, with a tendency for mergers to increase over time.

The book industry will not disappear—humanity would not survive without the written word. However, it remains to be seen what form those words will take. The structure of the book industry will continue to evolve along with the technologies that shape it and propel it forward.

References

Alterman, Jack, and Eva E. Jacobs, "Estimates of Real Output in the United States by Industrial Sector, 1947–1955," in *Output, Input and Productivity Measurement*, Studies in Income and Wealth, Vol. 25, NBER (Princeton, N. J.: Princeton University Press, 1961, 275–315).

Arrow, Kenneth, "The Theory of Risk Aversion," in *Collected Papers of Kenneth J. Arrow: Individual Choice under Certainty and Uncertainty*, Vol. 3 (Cambridge, Mass.: Belknap Press of Harvard University Press, 1984, 147–171).

Arrow, Kenneth, *Collected Papers of Kenneth J. Arrow: Production and Capital*, Vol. 5 (Cambridge, Mass.: Belknap Press of Harvard University Press, 1985).

Arrow, Kenneth, H. B. Chenery, B. S. Minhas, and R. M. Solow, "Capital-Labor Substitution and Economic Efficiency," *Review of Economics and Statistics*, Vol. 43, No. 196, 1961, 225–250.

Arrow, Kenneth, Samuel Karlin, and Herbert Scarf, *Studies in the Mathematical Theory of Inventory and Production* (Stanford, Calif.: Stanford University Press, 1958, 16–36).

Association of American Publishers, Inc (AAP), "Book Sales Total $25 Billion in 2000," February 28, 2001. Available from http://www.publishers.org.

Association of American Publishers, Inc (AAP), "Book Sales Total $25 Billion in 2001," March 1, 2002. Available from http://www.publishers.org.

Association of American Publishers, Inc (AAP), "Contractual Licensing, Technological Measures and Copyright Law" (WWW. Publishers. org/confpub/index.htm), 2002, 1–13.

Bailey, Joseph, P., "Intermediation and the Electronic Market: Aggregation and Pricing in Internet Commerce," PhD dissertation, MIT, 1998.

Bain, J., "Relation of Profit Rate to Industry Concentration: American Manufacturing. 1936 – 1940," *Quarterly Journal of Economics*, Vol. 65, 1951, 293–324.

Bain, J., *Industrial Organization* (New York: John Wiley, 1956).

Balassa, Bela., "A Changing Pattern of Comparative Advantage in Manufactured Goods," *The Review of Economics and Statistics*, Vol. 61, No. 2, May 1979, 259–266.

Baldwin, Robert E., "Determinants of the Commodity Structure of U. S. Trade," *American Economic Review*, Vol. 61, No. 1, March 1971, 126–146.

Baldwin, Robert E., "Determinants of the Commodity Structure of U. S. Trade: Reply," *American Economic Review*, Vol. 62, No. 3, June 1972, 465.

Becker, Gary S., *Human Capital*, Third Edition (Chicago, Ill.: University of Chicago Press, 1993).

Bekken, Jon, "Feeding the Dinosaurs: Economic Concentration in the Retail Book Industry," *Publishing Research Quarterly*, Vol. 13, No. 4, Winter 1997/1998, 1–26.

Bernstein, Paula, "Using Statistics: A Book Industry Case Study," *Searcher*, Vol. 13, No. 5, May 2005, 40–52.

Bettis, Richard A., and Kenan-Flagler, "Commentary on 'Redefining Industry Structure for the Information Age' by J. L Sampler," *Strategic Management Journal*, Vol. 19, 1998, 357–361.

Beynon, John and David Dunkerley (Eds.), *Globalization: The Reader* (New York: Routledge, 2000).

Bittlingmayer, G., "Resale Price Maintenance in the Book Trade with an Application to Germany," *Journal of Institutional and Theoretical Economics*, Vol. 44, No. 1, 1988, 789–812.

Bittlingmayer, G., "The Elasticity of Demand for Books, Resale Price Maintenance and the Lerner Index," *Journal of Institutional and Theoretical Economics*, Vol. 148, No. 4, 1992, 588–606.

Book Industry Trends 1999 (New York: Book Industry Study Group, 1999).

References

Book Industry Trends 2000 (New York: Book Industry Study Group, 2000).

Bowker Annual Library and Book Trade Almanac, edited by Dove Bogart and Julia C. Blixrud (Medford, N. J.: Information Today, 2011).

Brynjolfsson, Erick, "Commentary: High-Technology Industries and Market Structure," in Federal Reserve Bank of Kansas City (FRB), *Economic Policy for the Information Economy: A Symposium*, 2001, pp. 103–110.

Brynjolfsson, Erik and Adam Saunders, *Wired for Innovation* (Cambridge, Mass.: MIT Press, 2010).

Brynjolfsson, Erick and Lorin M. Hitt, "Beyond Computation: Information Technology, Organization Transformation and Business Performance," *Journal of Economic Perspectives*, Vol. 14, No. 4, Fall 2000, 23–48.

Brynjolfsson, Erik and Michael D. Smith, "Frictionless Commerce? A Comparison of Internet and Conventional Retailers, *Management Science*, Vol. 46, 2000, 563–585.

Brynjolfsson, Erik and Brian Kahin (Eds.), *Understanding the Digital Economy: Data, Tools, and Research* (Cambridge, Mass.: MIT Press, 2002 [2000]).

Brynjolfsson, Erik, Yu (Jeffrey) Hu, and Michael D. Smith, "Consumer Surplus in the Digital Economy: Estimating the Value of Increased Product Variety at Online Booksellers," *Management Science*, Vol. 49, No. 11, *Special Issue on E-Business and Management Science*, November 2003, 1580–1596.

Canoy, M. F. M. and van der Ploeg, Rick and van Ours, Jan C., "The Economics of Books, " Chapter 21 in *Handbook of the Economics of Art and Culture*, Vol. 1 (Holland: Elsevier, 2006, 721–761).

Carlsson, Bo, "The Digital Economy: What Is New and What Is Not?" *Structural Change and Economic Dynamics*, Vol. 15 (2004), 245–264.

Cave, Martin and Robin Mason, "The Economics of the Internet: Infrastructure and Regulation," *Oxford Review of Economic Policy*, Vol. 17, No. 2, 2001, 188–201.

Chamberlin, Edward H., *The Theory of Monopolistic Competition* (Cambridge, Mass.: Harvard University Press, 1962 [1933]).

Clay, Karen, Ramayya Krishnan and Erik Wolff, "Prices and Price Dispersion on the Web: Evidence from the Online Book Industry," *Journal of Industrial Economics*, Vol. 49, 2001, 521–540.

Clerides, Sofronis K., "Book Value: Intertemporal Pricing and Quality Discrimination in the US Market for Books," *International Journal of Industrial Organization*, Vol. 20, 2002, 1385–1408.

Cowhey, Peter F., and Jonathan D. Aronson, *Transforming Global Information Communication Markets* (Cambridge, Mass.: MIT Press, 2009).

Cox, Meg, "Booksellers Put Survival on Top Shelf as Superstores Vie for Tough Customers," *The Wall Street Journal*, May 26, 1991, 88.

Craft, N. F. R., and Mark Thomas, "Comparative Advantage in U. K. Manufacturing Trade, 1910–1935," *The Economic Journal*, Vol. 96, No. 282, September 1986, 629–645.

Cramer, J. S., Empirical Econometrics, (Amsterdam: North-Holland Publishing Co., 1971)

Crawford, Walt, "Paper Persists: Why Physical Library Collections Still Matters," Online: http://www.ampersandcom.com/GeorgeLeposky/crawford1.html, January 1998.

Curwen, Peter J., "The Economics of Academic Publishing in the U. K.," *The Journal of Industrial Economics*, March 1977, 161–175.

Daripa, Arup, and Sandeep Kapur, "Pricing on the Internet," *Oxford Review of Economic Policy*, Vol. 17, No. 2, 2001, 202–216.

David, Paul A., "The Evolving Accidental Information Super-Highway," *Oxford Review of Economic Policy*, Vol. 17, No. 2, 2001, 159–187.

Davidson, Paul, "A Keynesian View of the Relationship Between Accumulation, Money and the Money Wage-Rate," *The Economic Journal*, Vol. 79, No. 314 (June 1969), 300–323.

Dennis, Everette E., Craig L. LaMay, and Edward C. Pease, *Publishing Books* (New Brunswick, N. J.: Transaction, 1997).

Dicken, Peter, *Global Shifts*, Fifth Edition (New York: Guilford Press, 2007).

Dornbusch, Rudiger, Stanley Fischer, and Richard Startz, *Macroeconomics*, Ninth Edition (New York: McGraw-Hill and Irwin, 2004).

"EBOOKS: World Wide Read," *FT Expat*, December 1, 2002.

Elie, Lolis E., "A Career You Can Make Book On," *Black Enterprise*, Vol. 21, No. 7, February 1991.

Enders, Albrecht and Tawfik Jelassi, "The Converging Business Models of Internet and Bricks-and-Mortar Retailers," *European Management Journal*, Vol. 18, No. 5, 2000, 542–550.

Epstein, Jason, *Book Business: Publishing, Past, Present, and Future* (New York: W.W. Norton, 2001).

Farrington, Frank, *Meeting Chain Store Competition* (Chicago, Ill: Byxbee, 1922).

FCC, www.fcc.gov/wcb/iatd/trends.html: *Trends in Telephone Service: Industry Analysis and Technology Division Wireline Competition Bureau*, September 2010.

Federal Reserve Bank of Kansas City (FRB), "Economic Policy for the Information Economy: A Symposium," 2001.

Flores, Babur Ivan De Los Santos, "Consumer Search on the Internet," PhD Dissertation, University of Chicago, June 2008.

Fredriksson, Einar H. (Ed.), *A Century of Science Publishing* (Washington, D.C.: IOS Press, 2001).

Gale Research, *Encyclopedia of Global Industry*, 1996.

Gayer, Gayer and Oz Shy, "Internet and Peer-to-Peer Distributions in Markets for Digital Products," *Economics Letters*, Vol. 81, 2003, 197–203.

Ghosemajumder, Shuman, *Advanced Peer-Based Technology Business Models* (Cambridge, Mass.: MIT Sloan School of Management, 2002)

Gibbons, Michael (Ed.), *The New Production of Knowledge: Dynamics of Science and Research in Contemporary Societies* (Thousand Oaks, CA: Sage, 2004).

Gordon, Robert J., "Does the 'New Economy' Measure up to the Great Inventions of the Past?" *Journal of Economic Perspectives*, Vol. 14, No. 4, Fall 2000, 49–74.

Greco, Albert N., "Shaping the Future: Mergers, Acquisitions, and the U.S. Publishing, Communications, and Mass Media Industries, 1990–1995," *Publishing Research Quarterly*, 1996, 5–15.

Greco, Albert N., *The Book Publishing Industry*, (London, U. K.: Allyn and Bacon, 1997).

Greco, Albert N., *The Book Publishing Industry* (New York: Lawrence Earlbaum Associates, 2004).

Greco, Albert N., *The Book Publishing Industry*, Second Edition (New York: Lawrence Erlbaum Associates, 2005).

Greene, William H., *Econometric Analysis*, Third Edition (Upper Saddle River, N.J.: Prentice Hall, 1997).

Greene, William H., *Econometric Analysis*, Fourth Edition (New York: Wiley, 2000).

Gylfason, Thorvaldur, *Principles of Economic Growth* (Oxford: Oxford University Press, 2003).

Hay, Donald A., and Derek J. Morris, *Industrial Economics: Theory and Evidence* (Oxford: Oxford University Press, 1979).

He, Linhai, "Pricing Internet Services," PhD Dissertation, University of California, Berkeley, 2004.

Helpman, Elhanan (Ed.), *General Purpose Technologies and Economic Growth* (Cambridge, Mass.: MIT Press, 1998).

Helpman, Elhanan (Ed.), *Understanding Global Trade* (Cambridge, Mass.: Harvard University Press, 2011).

Hertel, T. W., *Global Trade Analysis: Modeling and Applications* (Cambridge: Cambridge University Press. 1997).

Hong, Han and Matthew Shum, "Using Price Distributions to Estimate Search Costs, *RAND Journal of Economics,* Vol. 37, No. 2, Summer 2006, 257–275.

Hotelling, Harold, "Stability in Competition," *Economic Journal,* Vol. 39, 1929, 41–57.

Hubbard, R. Glenn and Anthony Patrick O'brien, *Microeconomics,* Third Edition (New York: Prentice Hall, 2010).

Jones, Margaret, "Mergers-and-Acquisitions Aftershocks," *Publishers Weekly,* September 20, 1999.

Keynes, John Maynard, *The General Theory of Employment, Interest and Money* (Cambridge: Cambridge University Press for the Royal Economic Society, 1936).

Krugman, Paul R., *Rethinking International Trade* (Cambridge, Mass.: MIT Press, 1994).

Laffront, Jean-Jacques and Jean Tirole, *Competition in Telecommunications* (Cambridge, Mass.: MIT Press, 2002 [2000]).

Latcovich, Simon and Howard Smith, "Pricing, Sunk Costs, and Market Structure Online: Evidence from Book Retailing," *Oxford Review of Economic Policy,* Vol. 17, No. 2, 2001, 217–234.

Lee, Eric Y., and Michael Szenberg, "Analysis of Factors Determining Book Consumption in the United States, 1952–1985," in Douglas V. Shaw, William S. Hendon, and Virginia Lee Owen, eds., *Cultural Economics, An American Perspective* (Akron, OH: Association for Cultural Economics, 1990).

Levine-Clark, Michael, "An Analysis of Used-Book Availability on the Internet," *Library Collections, Acquisitions, & Technical Services,* Vol. 28, 2004, 283–297.

Lucas, Robert E. Jr., *Lectures on Economic Growth*, (Cambridge, Mass.: Harvard University Press, 2000).

Lucas, Robert E., Jr., *Lectures on Economic Growth* (Cambridge, Mass.: Harvard University Press, 2002).

MacKie-Mason, Jeffrey K., and Hal Varian, "Economic FAQs About the Internet," *The Journal of Economic Perspectives*, Vol. 8, No. 3, Summer 1994, 75–96.

Machlup, Fritz, *The Production and Distribution of Knowledge in the United States* (Princeton, N. J.: Princeton University Press, 1962).

Machlup, Fritz, "Publishing Scholarly Books and Journals: Is It Economically Viable?" *The Journal of Political Economy*, Vol. 85, No. 1, February 1977, 217–225.

Manes, Stephen, "Gutenberg Need Not Worry—Yet," *Forbes*, February 8, 1999.

Mann, Thomas, "The Importance of Books, Free Access, and Libraries as places—and the Dangerous Inadequacy of the Information Science Paradigm," *The Journal of Academic Librarianship*, Vol. 27, No. 4, July 2001, 268–221.

Marshall, Alfred, *Principles of Economics*, Eighth Edition (London: Macmillan, 1982 [1890]).

Marshall, Alfred,*The Correspondence of Alfred Marshall: Volume Three: Towards the Close, 1903-1924*, edited by John K. Whitaker (Cambridge: Cambridge University Press, 1996).

Maryles, Daisy, "They're the Tops!" *Publishers Weekly*, January 4, 1999.

Miller, Laura J., *Reluctant Capitalists: Bookselling and the Culture of Consumption* (Chicago, Ill.: University of Chicago Press, 2006).

Milliot, Jim, "Good Times Returning for Children's Publishing?," *Publishers Weekly*, February 22, 1999.

Milliot, Jim, "News Corp. to Acquire Morrow, Avon from Hearst," *Publishers Weekly*, June 21, 1999.

Milliot, Jim, "Salary Survey," *Publishers Weekly*, July 5, 1999.

Milliot, Jim, "Salary Survey: Amid Tight Job Market, Average Raise Fell in 2001," *Publishers Weekly*, July 8, 2002.

Milliot, Jim, and John F. Baker. "IDG Books Buys Macmillan General Reference," *Publishers Weekly*, July 5, 1999.

Merton, Robert C., "Analytical Optimal Control Theory as Applied to Stochastic and Non-Stochastic Economics," PhD Dissertation, MIT, 1970.

Merton, Robert C., "Paul Samuelson and Financial Economics," in Michael Szenberg, Lall Ramrattan, and Aron A. Gottesman, *Samuelsonian Economics and the Twenty-First Century* (Oxford: Oxford University Press, 2006, 262–300).

Morgan-Stanley, *The Internet Retailing Report*, May 28, 1997.

Mortimer, Richard Allen, "Investment and Cooperation among Internet Backbone Firms," Unpublished PhD Dissertation at University of California, Berkeley, 2001.

Morton, Robert C., "Analytical Optimal Control Theory as Applied to Stochastic and Non-Stochastic Economics," (Cambridge, Mass.: M.I.T. Ph.D. dissertation, 1970).

Mutter, John, "The Inevitable Future," *Publishers Weekly*, November 15, 1999.

O'Brian, Jeffrey M., "Amazon's Next Revolution," Fortune, June 8, 2009, 70–76.

Ostapenko, Nikolai, "Marketing Strategies of Selling Electronic Books in China," Heinz Sarkowski, "The Growth and Decline of German Scientific Publishing 1850—*International Journal of Advances in Management Science*, 2012, 1–6, Published Online, July 2012.

Pearce, Lynn (Ed.), "SIC 2731 Book Publishing," *Encyclopedia of American Industries, Volume One: Manufacturing Industries*. Fourth Edition (Detroit: Gale, 2005, 409–416).

Pearce, Lynn (Ed.), *Manufacturing Industries*. Fourth Edition (Detroit: Gale, 2005, 409–416).

Pearce, Lynn (Ed.), *Gale Virtual Reference Library*, 2 vols. (San Francisco Public Library, Gale, June 16, 2009).

Peters, Jean, "Book Industry Statistics from the R. R. Bowker Compny," *Publishing Research Quarterly*, Vol. 8, Fall 1992, 18.

Porter, Michael E., *The Competitive Advantage of Nations* (New York: Free Press, 1990).

Ramrattan, Lall and Michael Szenberg, *Distressed US Industries in the Era of Globalization* (Burlington, VT: Ashgate, 2007).

Reinert, Kenneth A., *Windows on the World Economy* (Mason, Ohio: South-Western, 2005).

Roback, Diane, "Licensed Tie-ins Make Registers Ring," *Publishers Weekly*, March 29, 1999.

Robinson, Joan, *The Economics of Imperfect Competition* (London: Macmillan, 1933).

Romer, Paul M., "Endogenous Technological Change," *Journal of Political Economy*, Vol. 98, No. 5, Part 2: The Problem of Development: A Conference of the Institute for the Study of Free Enterprise Systems (Oct., 1990), S71–S102.

Romer, Paul, "Bank of America Roundtable on the Soft Revolution: Achieving Growth by Managing Intangibles," *Journal of Applied Corporate Finance*, Vol. 11, No. 2, 1998, 8–27.

Ronte, Honna, "The Impact of Technology on Publishing," *Publishing Research Quarterly*, Vol. 16, No. 44, Winter 2001, 11–22.

Samuelson, Paul A., *Foundations of Economic Analysis*, Harvard Economic Studies, Vol. 80, 1947; references are to the seventh reprint edition, 1974, by Atheneum, New York.

Samuelson, Paul A., *The Collected Scientific Papers of Paul A. Samuelson*, edited by Joseph E. Stiglitz, Vols. 1 and 2 (Cambridge, Mass.: MIT Press, 1966).

Samuelson, Paul, *The Collected Scientific Papers of Paul A. Samuelson*, edited by Robert C. Merton, Volume 3 (Cambridge, Mass.: The M.I.T. Press, 1972).

Samuelson, Paul A., *The Collected Scientific Papers of Paul A. Samuelson*, edited by Robert C. Merton, Vol. 3 (Cambridge, MA: MIT Press, 1986).

Samuelson, Paul A., *The Collected Scientific Papers of Paul A. Samuelson*, edited by H. Nagatani and K. Cowley, Vol. 4 (Cambridge, MA: MIT Press, 1986).

Samuelson, Paul A., *The Collected Scientific Papers of Paul A. Samuelson*, edited by Kate Crowley, Vol. 5 (Cambridge, MA: MIT Press, 1986).

Samuelson, Paul A., *The Collected Scientific Papers of Paul A. Samuelson*, edited by Janice Murray, Vol. 6 (Cambridge, MA: MIT Press, 2011).

Samuelson, Paul A., *The Collected Scientific Papers of Paul A. Samuelson*, edited by Janice Murray, Vol. 7 (Cambridge, MA: MIT Press, 2011).

Santos, Babur De los, Ali Hortacsu, and Matthijs R. Wildenbeest, "Testing Models of Consumer Search Using Data on Web Browsing and Purchasing Behavior," Working Paper #09-23, September 2009, http://ssrn.com/abstract=1483380.

Sargent, Thomas J., *Dynamic Macroeconomic Theory* (Cambridge, Mass.: Harvard University Press, 1987).

Sarkowski, Heinz, "The Growth and Decline of German Scientific Publishing 1850–1945," in *A Century of Science Publishing*, edited by E. H. Fredricksson (Amsterdam, The Netherlands: IOS Press 2001, 25–34).

Schumpeter, Joseph A., *Capitalism, Socialism, and Democracy*, (New York: Harper and Brothers, 1942).

Schwartzman, David, "Production and Productivity in the Service Industries," in *Studies in Income and Wealth, NBER Conference on Research in Income and Wealth*, edited by Victor R. Fuchs, Vol. 34, 1969, 201–230.

Schwartzman, David, *The Decline of Service in Retail Trade: An Analysis of the Growth of Sales per Man-Hour, 1919–1963* (Pullman, WA: Washington State University Press, 1971).

Scotchmer, Suzanne, *Innovation and Incentives* (Cambridge, Mass.: MIT Press, 2004).

Selten, Reinhard, "The Chain Store Paradox," *Theory and Decision*, Vol. 9, No. 2, 1978, 127–159.

Shapiro, Carl and Hal Varian, *Information Rules: A Strategic Guide to the Network Economy* (Cambridge, Mass.: Harvard Business School Press, 1999).

Shatzkin, Mike, "Fasten Your High-Tech Seatbelts," *Publishers Weekly*, May 24, 1999.

Standard & Poor's Industry Surveys: Publishing. New York: Standard & Poor's Corporation, October 14, 1999.

Smith, Adam, *The Glasgow Edition of the Works and Correspondence of Adam Smith*, edited by R. H. Campbell, A. S. Skinner, and W. B. Todd, (Oxford, U. K.: Clarendon Press, 1976).
Volume I: The Theory of Moral Sentiments (TMS).
Volume II: An Inquiry into the Nature and Causes of The Wealth of Nations (WN).
Volume V: Lectures on Jurisprudence (LP) (Oxford, U. K.: Oxford University Press, 1978).

Smith, Michael D., Joseph Bailey, and Erik Brynjolfsson, "Understanding Digital Markets: Review and Assessment," in *Understanding the Digital Economy: Data, Tools, and Research*, edited by Erik Brynjolfsson and Brian Kahin (Cambridge, Mass.: MIT Press, 2002, [2000]), 99–137.

Smith, Roysce, "One-Third of the Sales, 85% of the Paperwork," *Publisher's Weekly*, August 7, 1967, 36.

Solow, Robert M., "Technical Change and the Aggregate Production Function," *The Review of Economics and Statistics*, Vol. 39, August 1957, 312–320.

Standard & Poor's "Industry Survey," July 1995, M89.

Stigler, George J., "The Economics of Information," *The Journal of Political Economy*, Vol. 69, No. 2 (June 1961), 213–225.

Stigler, George J., *The Organization of Industry* (Chicago, Ill.: University of Chicago Press, 1968).

Stigler, George J., *Essays in the History of Economics* (Chicago, Ill.: University of Chicago Press, 1995).

Stiglitz, Joseph E., "Information and Economic Analysis: A Perspective," *The Economic Journal*, Vol. 95, Supplement: Conference Papers, 1985, 21–41.

Stiglitz, Joseph E., "On the Market for Principles of Economics Textbooks: Innovation and Product Differentiation," *The Journal of Economic Education*, Vol. 19, No. 2, Spring 1988, 171–177.

Stiglitz, Joseph E., *Selected Works, Volume I: Information and Economic Analysis* (Oxford: Oxford University Press, 2009).

Studenmund, A. H., *Using Econometrics*, Third Edition (New York: Addison-Wesley, 1997).

Szenberg, Michael, "Disseminating Scholarly Output: The Case for Eliminating the Exclusivity of Journal Submissions," *The American Journal of Economics and Sociology*, July 1994, 303–315.

Szenberg, Michael and Eric Y. Lee, "The Structure of the American Book Publishing Industry," *Journal of Cultural Economics*, Vol. 18, 1994, 313–322.

Szenberg, Michael and Lall Ramrattan, *Franco Modigliani: A Mind That Never Rests* (New York: Palgrave Macmillan, 2008)

Tatlock, Lynne (Ed.), *Publishing Culture and the "Reading Nation": German Book History in the Nineteenth Long Century* (New York: Camden House, 2010).

"The 60-Second Book: A New High-Tech Publishing Technique Is Creating a Literary Big Bang for America's Would-Be Authors," *Time*, August 2, 1999.

US Department of Commerce, *Industry and Trade Outlook 2000* (Washington, D.C.: Government Printing Office, 2001).

Varian, Hal R., "Market Structure in the Network Age," in *Understanding the Digital Economy: Data, Tools, and Research*, edited by Erik Brynjolfsson and Brian Kahin (Cambridge, Mass.: MIT Press, 2002, [2000a]), 137–150.

Varian, Hal R., "Buying, Sharing and Renting Information Goods," *The Journal of Industrial Economics*, Vol. 48, No. 4, December 2000b, 473–488.

Varian, Hal R., " High-Technology Industries and Market Structure," in Federal Reserve Bank of Kansas City (FRB), *Economic Policy for the Information Economy: A Symposium*," 2001, 65–102.

Varian, Hal R., *The Economics of Information Technology: An Introduction* (Cambridge: Cambridge University Press, 2004).

Viscusi, Kip W., Joseph E. Harrington, Jr., and John M. Vernon, *Economics of Regulation and Antitrust*, Fourth Edition (Cambridge, Mass.: MIT Press, 2005).

Waldman, Don E., and Elizabeth J. Jensen, *Industrial Organization: Theory and Practice*, Third Edition (New York: Pearson-Addison Wesley, 2007).

Walker, Peter, "Explaining the Characteristics of the Power (CARRA) Utility Family," *Health Economics*, Vol. 17, 2008, 1329–1344.

Wallis, Kenneth F., *Topics in Applied Econometrics*, (London, U. K.: Gray-Mills Publishing LTD, 1973).

Wan, Minhua, *Demand Uncertainty, Search Cost and Price Dispersion: Evidence from the Online Book Industry*, PhD Dissertation, University of Chicago, June 2006.

"What's New with... Textbooks and Technology," *Technology & Learning*, May 1999.

Wildenbeest, Matthijs, "Market Characteristics, Consumers' Search Intensity and Competitiveness," Master Thesis, Erasmus University Rotterdam, Supervisor: Dr. Jose Luis Moraga, June 9, 2003.

"Wiley Buys Pearson College Titles," *Publishers Weekly*, May 24, 1999.

Wright, Garvin, "The Origins of American Industrial Success, 1989–1940," *American Economic Review*, Vol.80, No. 4, September 1990, 651–668.

"Store Count, E-Commerce Top Priorities," *Discount Store News*, August 9, 1999.

"YTD College Textbook Sales Remain High," *Educational Marketer*, October 14, 2002.

Zeitchik, Steve, "Mission Possible: Expand the Market; with Unit Sales Slipping, Industry Members Try New Ways to Find New Readers—and Book Buyers (Outlook 2003: The Hunt for New Readers)," *Publishers Weekly*, January 6, 2003.

Index

Adams, Walter, 2
Adverse selection, 48
Advertising Rivalry Hypothesis, 14
Amazon, vi, 6, 8–14, 16, 17, 21, 27, 28, 37–40, 44, 46, 54, 79, 95, 124, 127, 130, 132, *See* Amazon.com
Amazon.com, 6, 8–10, 16, 27, 44, 46, 79, 95, 127
American Booksellers Association, 42
Area of Dominant Influence, 43
Asia, 5, 65, 109, 111–113, 115, 116, 118, 119, 132

Bailey, Joseph J., 20
Bailey, Joseph P., 22
Bain, Joe, 26, 96, 133
Barnes & Noble, 6, 9, 10, 12–17, 21, 23, 25, 27, 28, 37, 39–41, 43, 44, 46, 80, 95, 124, 127, 130, 132
Bernstein, Paula, 51
Bittlingmayer, George, 54
Books-a-Million, xii, 6, 9, 11–15, 17, 37, 39, 40, 44, 47, 80, 95, 132
Borders, vii, xi, 4, 6, 9–11, 13–17, 28, 32, 39, 43, 44, 95, 133
Brock, James, 2

Chamberlin, Edward, 26

China, 5, 9, 65, 111, 115, 117–119, 132
competitive discounting, 36, 38
Crawford, Walt, 53

demand and supply, xi, 8, 27, 32, 44, 45, 49
Dionne, Joseph, 75
dynamic programming, 24, 38, 45, 132

e-books, x, xi, 2, 4, 9, 10, 27, 28, 32, 37, 38, 44
Economies of Scale, 24
Elie, Lolis Eric, 97
Endogenous Growth, 46
Europe, iv, 5, 109, 111, 112, 118, 119, 132
Exogenous Growth, 46

Franchising Rivalry Hypothesis, 14

game theory, xi, 24, 41
Gayer, Amit, 126
Germany, 5, 9, 39, 115, 117, 119, 127, 132
Gibbons, 38
the Great Recession, 16, 48, 113
Greco, Albert, 52, 95
Gylfason, 29, 46

Hertel, 113
Hong and Shum, 36

Index

Hotelling, Harold, 26

imperfect information, 47
Information Flow, 47
Internet Backbone Providers, 124
Internet Service Providers, 124

Keynes, John Maynard, 31, 110

Latcovich and Smith, 23
life cycle hypothesis, 58

Mann, Thomas, 53
Marshall, Alfred, 29, 53, 80
Matchlup, Fritz, 101
Microsoft, 37, 48
Miller, 42

Nicole, Pierre, x
non-price competition, xi, 2, 4, 19, 20, 23, 27, 60
North America, 5, 9, 109, 112, 115, 116, 118, 119, 132

Peters, Jean, 7
Porter, Michael, 126
price competition, 3, 4, 19–21, 23
price discrimination, 20, 37, 42
price dispersion, 19, 21, 23

R & D Rivalry Hypothesis, 15
reading for pleasure, 44
Ricardo, David, 121
Risk tolerance, 33

Rival Behavior, 11
Robinson, Joan, 26
Robinson-Patman Act, 43
Romer, Paul, 46, 121

Samuelson, Paul, 29, 32, 33
Sargent, Thomas, 30
Schumpeter, Joseph, 58, 121
Schwartzman, David, 7
Scotchmer, Suzanne, 20
Selten, Reinhard, 41
Shapiro and Varian, 20, 26
shop bots, 34
short-term fluctuations, 51
Shy, Oz, 126
smart market strategy, 21
Smith, Adam, ix, xiii, 36
Soros, George, 39
Stigler, George, xiv, 23, 34, 80, 96, 97, 99, 100
Stiglitz, Joseph, 26, 47, 80, 133
Strahan, William, ix
Studenmund, A.H., 79

Tatlock, Lynne, 117
technological shocks, 2, 28

Varian, Hal, 20
Vernon, Raymond, 58
Vickrey auction, 21, 24
Vickrey, William, 21

zero price strategy, 48
zero-sum game, xi, 2, 27, 28

GPSR Compliance

The European Union's (EU) General Product Safety Regulation (GPSR) is a set of rules that requires consumer products to be safe and our obligations to ensure this.

If you have any concerns about our products, you can contact us on

ProductSafety@springernature.com

In case Publisher is established outside the EU, the EU authorized representative is:

Springer Nature Customer Service Center GmbH
Europaplatz 3
69115 Heidelberg, Germany

www.ingramcontent.com/pod-product-compliance
Lightning Source LLC
LaVergne TN
LVHW041955060526
838200LV00002B/28